I0120736

Anonymous

**Norwich, Connecticut**

Its importance as a business and manufacturing centre and as a place of residence

Anonymous

**Norwich, Connecticut**
*Its importance as a business and manufacturing centre and as a place of residence*

ISBN/EAN: 9783337430368

Printed in Europe, USA, Canada, Australia, Japan

Cover: Foto ©Suzi / pixelio.de

More available books at **www.hansebooks.com**

VIEW OF HARBOR, NORWICH, CONN.

# NORWICH,

## CONNECTICUT:

## ITS IMPORTANCE AS A BUSINESS AND MANUFACTURING CENTRE AND AS A PLACE OF RESIDENCE.

---

## *A Brief Review of Its Past and Present.*

---

ISSUED BY

### THE NORWICH BOARD OF TRADE,

JANUARY, 1888.

NORWICH:
PRESS OF THE BULLETIN COMPANY.
1888.

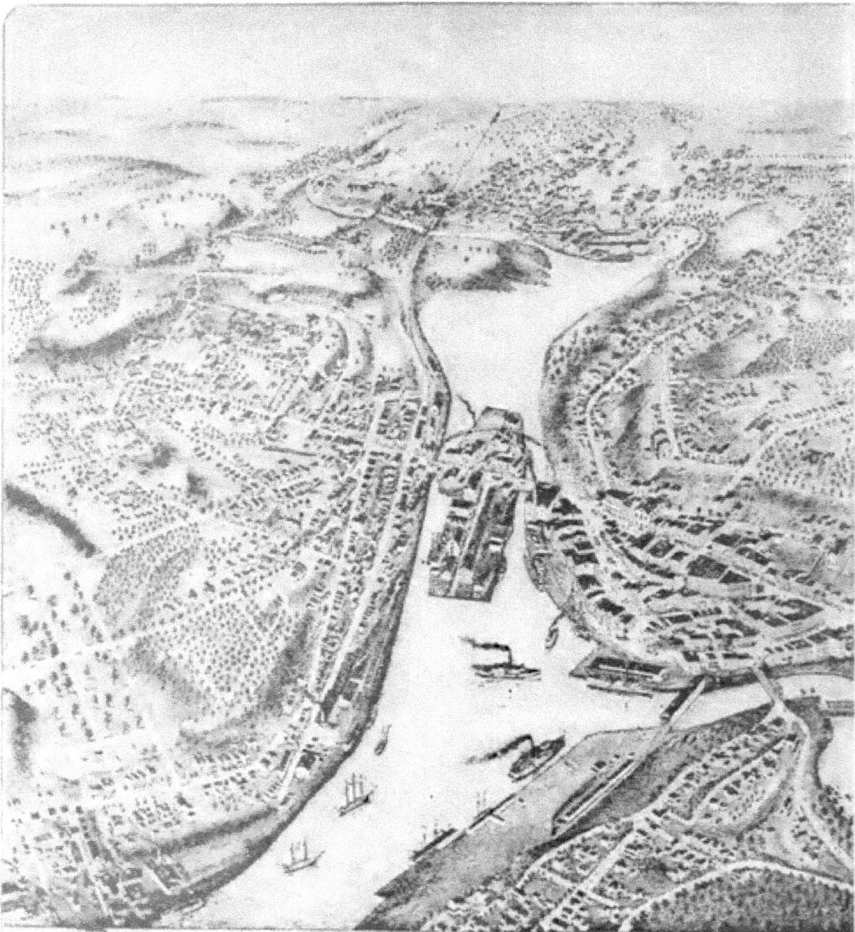

CITY OF Norwich 1876

# OFFICERS OF THE NORWICH BOARD OF TRADE.

**President,**

HUGH H. OSGOOD.

**Vice Presidents,**

E. WINSLOW WILLIAMS.
Dr. PATRICK CASSIDY,
FRANK A. MITCHELL.

**Recording Secretary,**

CHARLES E. DYER.

**Corresponding Secretary,**

H. H. GALLUP.

**Treasurer,**

JONATHAN TRUMBULL.

**Executive Committee,**

H. H. OSGOOD,

| | |
|---|---|
| E. WINSLOW WILLIAMS, | PATRICK CASSIDY, |
| FRANK A. MITCHELL, | SOLOMON LUCAS, |
| EDWIN S. ELY, | WM. N. BLACKSTONE, |
| ADAMS P. CARROLL. | JAMES A. BROWN. |

## Committee on Trades and Manufactures.

AMOS W. PRENTICE,

THOMAS D. SAYLES,     CHARLES BARD,

WM. H. SHIELDS.     DANIEL M. LESTER

## Committee on Entertainments.

DAVID A. WELLS.

WM. A. AIKEN,     ARTHUR H. BREWER,

EDWARD N. GIBBS.     ARCHIBALD MITCHELL.

## Committee on Arbitration.

CHARLES BARD,

JEREMIAH J. DESMOND.     JAMES H. ARNOLD,

REUBEN S. BARTLETT,     WM. T. LANE.

## Committee on Transportation.

HENRY H. GALLUP,

CHARLES E. DYER.     JOHN H. CRANSTON

ADAM REID.     WM. C. MOWRY.

## Committee on Statistics.

JOHN C. AVERILL,

BELA P. LEARNED,     JOHN T. BROWN,

FRANK J. LEAVENS,     S. ALPHEUS GILBERT.

# MEMBERS OF THE NORWICH BOARD OF TRADE.

| | |
|---|---|
| AIKEN, WM. A. | Prop. Norwich Nickel Works. |
| AVERILL, JOHN C. | Clerk Courts N. L. County. |
| ALMY, A. H. | Pres. Bozrah Mineral Spring Co. |
| ANDREWS, P. ST. M. | Superintendent N. & W. R. R. |
| ARNOLD, J. H. | Builder and Contractor. |
| | |
| BARBER, M. ANGELO | Machinist. |
| BARD, CHARLES | Receiver Hayward Rubber Co. |
| BLACKSTONE, J. D. T. | Cotton Manufacturer. |
| BLACKSTONE, WM. N. | Cotton Manufacturer. |
| BARSTOW, JOHN P. | Stoves and Farming Implements. |
| BREWER, ARTHUR H. | Coal and Lumber. |
| BROWN, JOHN T. | Agent Marvin Safe Co. |
| BREWER, J. M. | Druggist. |
| BUTTS, H. L. | File Manufacturer. |
| BISHOP, HERBERT M. | Physician. |
| BECKWITH, A. A. | Flour and Grain. |
| BROWNING, CHARLES D. | Groceries and Dry Goods. |
| BILL, HENRY | Book Publisher. |
| BRISCOE, WILLIS A. | Lawyer. |
| BROWN, JAMES A. | Wholesale Grocer. |
| BARTLETT, R. S. | Grocer. |
| BRAND, JUNIUS A. | Supt. Norwich Aqueduct Co. |
| BLIVEN, S. E. | Paper Box Manufacturer. |
| BEEBE, CHAS. H. | Treas. & M'ger Nor. Lock Mfg. Co. |
| BROWN, ROBERT | Plumber. |
| | |
| CARDWELL, W. H. | Grocer. |
| CARROLL, ADAMS P. | Cotton and Wool. |
| CARROLL, GEO. W. | Cotton and Wool. |

| | |
|---|---|
| CASSIDY, PATRICK | Physician. |
| CONGDON, GILBERT L. | Builder and Contractor. |
| CAMP, FREDERICK S. | Secretary Ponemah Mills. |
| CARPENTER, INCREASE W. | Mayor of Norwich. |
| CHANDLER, CHAS. E. | Surveyor and Civil Engineer. |
| CONVERSE, CHAS. A. | Pistol Manufacturer. |
| CRANSTON, J. H. | Printing Press Manufacturer. |
| CARROLL, L. W. | Cotton Manufacturer. |
| COGSWELL, CHAS. P. | Banker. |
| COIT, GEORGE D. | Treasurer Chelsea Savings Bank. |
| CAREY, A. E. | Builder and Contractor. |
| CHAPMAN, ENOCH F. | Coal and Lumber. |
| CRANDALL, S. A. | Lawyer. |
| COSGROVE, JAMES F. | Boots and Shoes. |
| CRANSTON, B. T. | Books and Stationery. |
| | |
| DESMOND, J. J. | Lawyer. |
| DUGGAN, JAMES | Druggist. |
| DAWSON, JR., JAMES | Meat Market. |
| DAY, NORMAN | Manufacturer. |
| DYER, CHARLES E. | Manager Norwich Bulletin. |
| DOWE, F. E. | Dry Goods. |
| DAVIS, C. H. | Wholesale Pork and Lard. |
| DAVIS, GEORGE A. | Books and Stationery. |
| | |
| ELY, WM. G. | Treas. Falls and Shetucket Mills. |
| ELY, EDWIN S. | Pres. Uncas Bank and Paper Mfr. |
| EATON, LUTHER S. | Hardware. |
| | |
| GOULD, GEO. W. | Manufacturer. |
| GIBBS, EDWARD N. | Cashier Thames National Bank. |
| GILBERT, S. ALPHEUS | Furniture and Carpets. |
| GALLUP, H. H. | Norwich Belt Manufacturing Co. |
| | |
| HARRIS, E. D. | Coal Dealer. |
| | |
| JEWETT, L. R. | Coal Dealer. |
| JOHNSON, FRANK | President Norwich National Bank. |
| JONES, DAVID R. | Merchant Tailor. |
| JOHNSON, JR., OLIVER L. | Treas. Norwich & N. Y. Trans. Co. |
| JOHNSON, CHARLES S. | Manufacturer. |

| | |
|---|---|
| KING, CHARLES J. | Flour, Meal and Hay. |
| KELLEY, JOHN H. | Boots, Shoes and Leather. |
| KEEP, JOHN H. | Book-keeper. |
| KINGSBURY, A. B. | Jeweler. |
| | |
| LEAVENS, FRANK J. | Cotton Manufacturer. |
| LEARNED, BELA P. | Insurance. |
| LUCAS, SOLOMON | Lawyer. |
| LESTER, D. M. | Mfr. of Envelope Machinery. |
| LANE, W. T. | Harness and Trunks. |
| LANE, GEO. A. | Harness and Trunks. |
| LATHROP, ARTHUR D. | Forwarding Agent. |
| | |
| MITCHELL, FRANK A. | Treas. Cold Spring Iron Works. |
| MITCHELL, ARCHIBALD | Dry Goods. |
| MITCHELL, A. G. | Sec. Cold Spring Iron Works. |
| MOWRY, WM. C. | Manufacturer Page Steam Heaters. |
| OSGOOD, HUGH H. | Drugs and Medicines. |
| | |
| PRENTICE, AMOS W. | Hardware. |
| PALMER, H. F. | Real Estate Agent. |
| PECK, SETH L. | Lime, Brick and Cement. |
| PRESTON, CHAS. H. | Hardware. |
| PAGE, WM. H. | Manufacturer Wood Type. |
| POTTER, A. L. | Coal. |
| PORTEOUS, JOHN | Dry Goods. |
| | |
| RAYMOND, GEO. C. | West India Trade. |
| ROYCE, A. IRVING | Insurance. |
| REID, ADAM | Dry Goods. |
| ROBBINS, Z. R. | Merchant. |
| RALLION, H. D. | Grocer. |
| | |
| SAYLES, THOS. D. | Woolen Manufacturer. |
| SMITH, A. D. | Merchant Tailor. |
| SNELL, DANIEL W. | Business College. |
| SHIELDS, WM. H. | Lawyer. |
| SMITH, J. HUNT | Treas. Dime Savings Bank. |
| SMITH, GEORGE S. | Franklin Steam Mills. |
| SMITH, FRANK H. | Stoves, Ranges, etc. |
| SMALL, NATHAN | Concrete Pavement and Roofing. |
| SHANNON, J. B. | Groceries. |

| | |
|---|---|
| TARRANT, NICHOLAS | Real Estate Agent. |
| TRUMBULL, JONATHAN | West India Trade. |
| TURNER, SIDNEY | President Norwich Lock Mfg. Co. |
| TURNER, F. C. | Secretary Ossawan Mills. |
| TUCKER, WM. C. | Superintendent Ponemah Mills. |
| TYLER, FRED. C. | Teas, Coffees and Spices. |
| | |
| ULMER, FRANK | Norwich Belt Co. |
| | |
| WELLS, DAVID A. | Political Economist. |
| WILLIAMS, E. WINSLOW | Woolen Manufacturer. |
| WILLIAMS, WINSLOW T. | Secretary Yantic Woolen Co. |
| WILLIAMS, JEROME F. | Insurance. |
| WHITTEMORE, M. M. | Clerk N. & W. R. R. Co. |
| WOODARD, F. L. | Asst. Treas. Dime Savings Bank. |
| WARNER, J. E. | Sec'y Hopkins & Allen Mfg. Co. |
| WASLEY, F. R. | Mfr. Envelope Machinery. |
| WINTERS, CHAS. J. | Dealer Chicago Dressed Beef. |
| WORTHINGTON, E. B. | Teas, Coffees and Spices. |

# BY WAY OF INTRODUCTION.

By referring to the constitution and by-laws of the NORWICH BOARD OF TRADE, it will be seen that the object of the organization is for " the advancement of the individual and general business interests of the community; the encouragement of commercial and manufacturing industries; the improvement of facilities for transportation; the diffusion of information concerning trades, manufacturing, and other interests; the cultivation of a more intimate knowledge of all events and questions affecting the public welfare," etc.

It is with the desire of promoting and encouraging the interests above enumerated that the following pages of statistical and local information are given to the public. Much care has been taken in the preparation of the work to confine all statements and figures within conservative bounds, the sole object being to present a true picture of Norwich as it is to-day, with its splendid educational facilities, its business interests, its importance as a manufacturing centre, its reputation as a healthy city, and various important subjects that make a place attractive, in order that strangers and intelligent inquirers may fully realize the great advantages of this locality as a place of residence, as well as a desirable field for locating manufactories of various kinds.

Schools, Churches, Public Libraries, Police and Fire Departments, Water Supply, Sewerage, Street Railways, Gas and Electric Light, Banks and Banking, Post Office Statistics, Cotton and Wool Trade, Coal and Lumber Trade, Railroad and Steamboat Freights, Tonnage of Thames River, Mill Privileges to be utilized, and various important matters are briefly mentioned in connection with the long array of statistical information that is given of Norwich industries, and of industries that are tributary to Norwich in the neighboring towns.

# NORWICH: PAST AND PRESENT.

The early history of Norwich, like that of many other of the old New England cities, reads more like a romance at the present day than a reality. It is difficult to conceive that where now stands its beautiful and palatial dwellings and public buildings, its fine ware-houses and stores, its busy manufactories, and its miles of streets teeming with a busy population, was once the home and hunting grounds of the Indian, without the first vestige of civilization. The city, which now has the reputation of being one of the most romantic and beautiful in New England, was first settled in 1659, by a small party of emigrants, led by Captain John Mason, who afterwards became famous as a leader and an officer in the Pequot and Mohegan wars.

For a long number of years it was a cheerless, dreary home for the white men who had built their log-houses amidst the treacherous savages, and where their lives were in constant peril from the nomadic tribes, who were jealous of the intrusion on their hunting grounds. But they had come to stay, and gradually, as years rolled by, increased in population and importance. As early as 1732, the town which they had founded was made a half-shire town, and in 1781, was one of the five incorporated cities of the State.

The city is romantically situated at the head of the river Thames, fourteen miles above Long Island Sound, at the junction of the Yantic and Shetucket rivers, and at the head of tide-water. As the city is approached from the river below, a high, rocky bluff presents itself—its base encircled by stores and ware-houses, while rising one above another to the rocky eminences which overhangs the business portion of the city, are zig-zag streets, cut out of solid rock like Alpine roads, on which are located the churches, public buildings and handsome private residences.

The growth of the city has been substantial, though neither slow or rapid. In the year 1800, the grand list of the town was $1,797,879; in 1825, $2,200,000; in 1850, $4,446,480; in 1885, it had increased to the large amount of $13,157,869, to which should be added the sum of $14,682,856 of property, such as churches, public buildings, school-houses, etc., which are exempt from taxation.

In the year 1821, Norwich had but 3,500 inhabitants; in 1870, according to the census taken then, there were 16,653; in 1880, by the census returns, there were 21,143. At this present time the increase must make the population in the immediate neighborhood of 25,000.

The city owes much of its prosperity to its commercial interests, and to its unsurpassed manufacturing facilities—having a fine harbor, easily accessible to large-size vessels drawing thirteen feet of water; and a very extensive water front, as well as excellent railroad privileges, being on the lines of the Norwich & Worcester Division of the New York & New England Railroad, and on the New London Northern Railroad. In addition to this, Norwich owes a large share of its growth to the splendid water-power privileges on the Shetucket, Yantic and Quinnebaug rivers, which flow through the town, and that have been utilized for manufacturing purposes by some of the largest mills in the country.

In its earlier days, Norwich was prominent among the few commercial cities of New England, on account of its shipping and ship building interests. As early as 1714, 1716 and 1722, the town granted rights to build ship-yards for ship-building purposes, giving the land and a free right to go into the forests and cut all the timber necessary to carry on the work. In 1788, Norwich exported 549 horses, 205 mules, 300 horned cattle, 321 sheep, 566 hogs, a large quantity of beef and pork, besides 30,000 lbs. of butter. In 1795, a large foreign trade was carried on with several European ports, especially with the West Indies, when the foundations of many Norwich fortunes were made. At that time, the shipping belonging to this port consisted of 7 ships—all over 200 tons burthen—9 brigs, 9 schooners, 17 sloops, besides a number of New York and river packets, the aggregate tonnage amounting to nearly 5,000 tons. From Captain Story's ship-yard, on the west side of the harbor, ships were launched of over 300 tons burthen.

Previous to the year 1817, travelers could only pass to or from New York by sail vessels or packets, which were advertised to make their weekly or monthly trips. The time occupied in making the passage varied according to the weather, and the direction from which the wind

was blowing—sometimes only a week, and often two and three would be used while becalmed, on encountering adverse winds. The passage was $5.00, with an additional $2.00 for "living;" but whether the "living" was regulated by an increase, with the contingency of a two or three weeks' trip, the writer knows not. There was, also, great rivalry and opposition between the owners and captains of the packets plying between the two cities, and many comical stories are told of the "arts and wiles" that were resorted to by them to obtain passengers and freight. The Norwich man in New York, with grip-sack in hand, eager to obtain passage to his "native heath" to rejoin his long anxious family, was often met by a crowd of importuning sailors belonging to the different rival packets, and often by the captains themselves, all clamoring for his patronage, and eager for his money. At such times opposition ran high, and if the Norwich man was keen and shrewd, as he generally was, the cost of his trip home was but a very small item of his expenses while absent. It is related that a goodly farmer from the neighboring town of Franklin, finding himself thus situated one afternoon in New York, about seventy years ago, commenced receiving bids of two rival packet masters to transport him to Norwich. Dollar by dollar they lowered their prices, until one of them agreed to bring him free, with no charge for "living;" but our economical and ancient neighbor finally accepted the offer of Captain Tyler, of the opposition packet, who not only agreed to bring him free, but to furnish him with free "grub" and free grog on the passage, and pay him fifty cents when the vessel reached Norwich—a promise that was religiously fulfilled on the application of the farmer for the money ere he stepped foot on shore.

In those days, the departure of a Norwich man for New York on business or pleasure—and they seldom went for the latter—was a great event, and of as much importance as it would be now for a man to start on a trip to Russia, or around the world. For weeks in advance, the matter was talked over and canvassed in the family circle, and preparations made for the perilous voyage. If he was a practical and methodical man, he made his will, in anticipation of contingencies of shipwreck, or being waylaid and murdered in the streets of New York; and his affairs were left in such a condition that they could be easily adjusted by an administrator in case he never returned. When the hour for his departure at last arrived, and he was to tear himself from his weeping family, the scene was as affecting and heart-rending as the separation of

John Rogers from his wife and nine little ones when he was burned at the stake.

In 1817, the first steamboat ploughed the waters of the river Thames, and some of the old inhabitants—and there are but few of them left—will well remember the first trip of the wonderful steamer "Fulton," Captain Bunker. As she moved away from the wharf at Norwich, smoke and flames belching forth from the smoke-stack, the revolving paddle-wheels lashing the heretofore quiet waters into an angry foam, the gallant captain walking the deck and giving orders with all the importance of a newly-appointed brigadier on muster day, it made a scene long remembered by the crowds of people that lined the adjacent shores and the wharf from which the marine monster made its departure. After the "Fulton," the steamer "H. E. Eckford," Captain Davison, was put on the route to New York, being replaced about 1827 by the "Fanny," with the same captain. In 1833, Captain Wm. W. Coit, once an honored resident, completed the "Jackson." Her first trip was to New London, with a large excursion party, on the occasion of laying the corner-stone of Groton Monument; and President Jackson, after whom the steamer was named, was the distinguished guest on board. In 1836, Captain Coit built the "Norwich," which he commanded till 1842, when the "Worcester," also built under the direction of this officer, took the place of the "Norwich." Soon after, it was deemed advisable to run two boats, on alternate days, and the "Charter Oak," Captain Sanford, was placed on the route.

Then came successively the "Knickerbocker," the "Connecticut," the ill-fated and beautiful steamers "Atlantic" and "Commonwealth,"—one wrecked on Fisher's Island, and the other destroyed by fire at the dock in Groton.

At present, the commodious steamers, "City of Worcester," "City of Boston," and "City of New York," together with the freight boats, "City of Lawrence," and "City of Norwich,"—the former carrying passengers as well as freight—connect Norwich with the great metropolis.

Among those early connected with the shipping interests of Norwich in the present century, and who contributed largely to its permanent establishment and success, Captain W. W. Coit, before referred to, ranks foremost. In the year 1817, when but nineteen years of age, he practically commenced his seafaring life, by going as master of the packet "McDonough," plying between Norwich and New York, touching at the

BROADWAY, NORWICH, CONN.

port of New London. He continued going as master of various packets until 1833, when the fruits of long years of toil and devoted attention to the duties of a mariner's life, enabled him to build and command the steamer " Jackson." During all the time that he had been connected with or commanded vessels propelled either by wind or steam, he proudly boasted—and well he might—that he had never lost a passenger, or a man, or a dollar's worth of freight or merchandise, by fire, accident or negligence. Can a similar record be produced?

During the memorable September gale, in 1815, Norwich suffered severely. The tide rose to an unprecedented height, submerged all what is now the business part of the city, destroying a large number of stores and ware-houses, and injuring many others. All the shipping in the harbor was driven ashore, and a large brig was left high and dry when the waters had receded, nearly opposite where now stands the grocery store of F. L. Gardner. The venerable drug store which stood on the ground now occupied by the handsome Tyler block, on Water Street, was nearly swept away by the rising tide ; but it stood its ground, though the waters reached the second floor. Many more incidents of great interest to the present generation might be spoken of relating to the NORWICH OF THE PAST, but limited space compels us to pass on, and speak of the NORWICH OF THE PRESENT.

# NORWICH MANUFACTORIES.

At a very early period in the history of Norwich the advantages of establishing manufactories of various kinds engaged a large share of the public attention, and the interest then taken in the subject gradually developed in the building of several large mills on the splendid water privileges that were in the town limits. Previous to 1840, Norwich was the largest manufacturing town in the State—the product of its mills in 1839, according to the report made to the Secretary of State, amounting to $1,150,205.00, which, in those days, was considered an enormous sum to be derived from such a source. Manufacturing at that time was in its infancy, compared to what it is at present. There was not then a steam engine probably in the whole town—the mill-owners depending entirely upon water power to drive their machinery. Below we give a list of the various manufactories that are in active operation in Norwich on the first of January of the present year, together with a few important but brief statistics connected therewith ; the number of hands employed in the many mills and work-shops; the aggregate amount paid annually for labor : the vast amount of yearly products ; the raw material consumed; the tons of freight handled, and various other items, will be a good deal of a surprise, not only to many of the inhabitants of Norwich, but to many outside its borders who may have imagined this to be a city chiefly celebrated for its beautiful residences, picturesque scenery, its unsurpassed educational facilities, its healthy climate, and its citizens depending upon retired wealth and outside interests for very many of the comforts as well as the necessities of life. As will be seen by referring to the statistics, 5,344 persons (more than one-fifth of the inhabitants) are employed in the manufactories, to whom $2,110,- 500.00 are paid annually for their labor. This large sum is constantly

ANNEX PONEMAH MILLS, (TAFTVILLE), NORWICH, CONN

changing hands in our midst. It supports our schools and churches ; it clothes the naked, and feeds the hungry; it enters the homes of the poor, as well as the rich, furnishing the necessities of life, as well as the luxuries and comforts.

The Ponemah Mill, which is said to be the second largest cotton mill in the world, has more employes than many of the towns in the state have inhabitants ; and the yards of cloth it annually manufactures, if spread out, would reach a distance of 11,364 miles, or nearly half round the world. The yards of cloth turned out by the Norwich Bleaching, Dyeing and Printing Company (28,409½ miles) would extend around the world, with about four thousand miles to spare. The enormous amount of goods turned out by these two mammoth concerns can only be appreciated by some such practical illustration as the above.

The statistics gathered from the various mills and manufactories have been furnished on personal application—with two or three exceptions— from the owners or managers themselves, and are as nearly correct as it is possible to get them, without too much time being spent in going over the ledgers and journals to arrive at exact amount of each. The figures given are about the general average, based upon the last year's expenditures and products. It is to be regretted that this aggregate of all the sales or products of the different manufactories could not be obtained, but this was found impossible, as many of the owners or proprietors preferred not to have the amount of their sales made public.

It is to be hoped that this remarkable showing which the many industries make, will be the means of inducing more of our capitalists and men of wealth to invest their money in home enterprises, instead of going abroad and investing in uncertain stocks and wildcat speculations. A good paying industry not only gives a fair return to investors, but it helps to build up a town, by increasing its wealth, adding to its population, and doubling the value of real estate. And no town in New England offers better advantages or facilities for manufacturing in its various branches than Norwich.

# COTTON MANUFACTORIES.

SINCE Norwich became prominent as a manufacturing town, which was over fifty years ago, the making of cotton fabrics has taken the precedence among its various industries. From 1823 to 1829, four joint stock companies were organized to manufacture cotton goods in connection with woolen goods, whose combined capital was limited to $1,530,000.00. Whether this capital was all employed, or whether the mills went into active operation, is doubtful ; but this cotton industry has continued to flourish from those years to the present, and has been the main source of the growth of the town. Three of the four cotton mills which are now in operation in Norwich have a combined capital of $2,500,000.00—the fourth, the Totokett, not being a joint stock company. The four mills employ 2,800 operatives, pay annually $810,-000.00 for labor, manufacture 34,500,000 yards goods, consume 8,650,-000 lbs. cotton, run 184,000 spindles. The Shetucket, Falls and Totokett mills handle annually 7,250 tons freight, and pay $49,000 freightage.

## THE PONEMAH COTTON MILLS.

This mammoth establishment is said to be the second largest cotton factory in the United States, if not in the world. It is situated on the Shetucket river, in the village of Taftville—a suburb of Norwich about 3½ miles from the centre of the city. The building of the dam and the mill was commenced in 1867, and the company commenced running the machinery in 1870. At that time there was not a house in sight of the privileges ; and where now stands a small city in appearance, with streets lined with handsome houses spreading out in various directions, there was but rocky, half-cultivated and neglected farming lands. The entire length of the mill, including a hundred-foot machine shop, is

FALLS COMPANY MILLS, NORWICH, CONN.

SHETUCKET COMPANY MILLS, NORWICH, CONN.

1,576 feet. Some idea of its vast size can be arrived at by stating that this number of feet makes the mill but a trifle less than a third of a mile long. It manufactures a fine quality of cotton goods, which find a ready market all over the country. The company owns 190 tenement houses, besides stores, store-houses, and various buildings connected with their manufactory.

| | |
|---|---|
| Capital stock | $1,500,000 |
| Bales cotton consumed per annum | 6,500 |
| Number of spindles | 125,000 |
| Yards goods made annually | 20,000,000 |
| Amount annually paid for labor | $ 450,000 |
| Number of hands employed | 1,300 |

## FALLS CO.

Next to the Ponemah Mills in size and importance are the Falls Company's Mills, situated at the Falls, so called, about half-a-mile from the business centre of the city, and within the city limits. The products of the mills are heavy, colored cotton goods, awnings, tickings, etc.

| | |
|---|---|
| Capital stock | $ 500,000 |
| Lbs. cotton consumed per annum | 2,600,000 |
| Yards colored goods manufactured per annum | 5,500,000 |
| Estimated lbs. of freight per annum | 6,000,000 |
| Number of spindles | 23,000 |
| Number of hands employed | 550 |
| Freights paid per annum | $ 24,000 |
| Amount annually paid for labor | $ 160,000 |

## THE SHETUCKET CO.

The mills of this large corporation for the manufacture of cotton goods, are situated at Greeneville, on the Shetucket river, a mile from city centre, and also in city limits.

| | |
|---|---|
| Capital stock | $ 500,000 |
| Lbs. cotton consumed per annum | 2,400,000 |
| Yards colored goods manufactured per annum | 6,000,000 |
| Estimated lbs. of freight per annum | 4,500,000 |
| Freights paid per annum | $ 22,000 |
| Number of spindles | 20,000 |
| Number of hands employed | 500 |
| Amount annually paid for labor | $ 130,000 |

## TOTOKETT MILLS.

Situated on the Shetucket river, 4½ miles from the centre of the City of Norwich, owned by Lorenzo Blackstone, and managed by his sons. They manufacture a fine quality of sheetings.

| | |
|---|---:|
| Number of spindles........................................ | 16,000 |
| Lbs. cotton consumed per annum............................ | 400,000 |
| Yards sheetings manufactured per annum.................... | 3,000,000 |
| Estimated lbs. of freight per annum....................... | 4,000,000 |
| Amount paid for freight per annum.....................$ | 5,000 |
| Amount paid for labor per annum.... ...................$ | 50,000 |
| Number of hands employed......... | 250 |

# WOOLEN MANUFACTORIES.

NEXT in importance to that of the cotton industry, which for a long number of years has been prominent as one of the sources of the city's growth and material prosperity, is that of the manufacture of woolen goods. At present, there are four mills engaged in this class of manufacture, the largest of which is that of the

## YANTIC WOOLEN COMPANY,

whose mills are on the Yantic river, in the village of the same name— another of the suburbs of our city. It manufactures a fine quality of flannels and ladies' dress goods.

| | |
|---|---:|
| Capital stock..............................................$ | 75,000 |
| Lbs. scoured wool consumed annually........................ | 430,000 |
| Yards flannel manufactured annually........................ | 2,250,000 |
| Tons of freight handled annually........................... | 2,100 |
| Amount paid freights annually..........................$ | 5,000 |
| Number setts of cards...................................... | 10½ |
| Number hands employed...................................... | 150 |
| Amount paid for labor per annum........................$ | 50,000 |

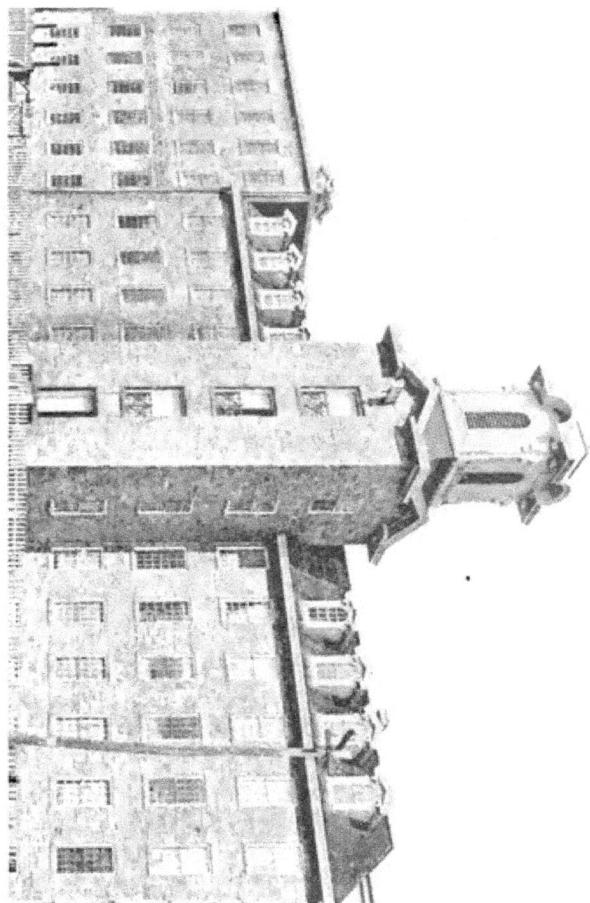

## NORWICH WOOLEN COMPANY

Located on the Yantic river, a mile-and-a-half north of the centre of the city, and make the manufacture of flannels a specialty.

Capital stock.................................................$ 100,000
Lbs. scoured wool consumed annually......................... 300,000
Number of hands employed.................................... 100
Amount annually paid for labor..............................$ 40,000
Setts of cards.............................................. 12

## THAMES VALLEY MILLS.

Located at Trading Cove, so called, a mile-and-a-half below the city, and at the outlet of Trading Cove brook.   It is owned and run by the Hall Brothers.

Lbs. unscoured wool annually consumed....................... 270,000
Yards flannel annually made................................. 350,000
Number of hands employed.................................... 50
Amount paid for labor per annum............................$ 12,000
Tons of freight handled..................................... 650

## CLINTON WOOLEN MILLS.

On the Yantic river, near Bean Hill, so called.   A joint stock company.

Capital stock..............................................$ 200,000
Number of hands employed.................................... 130
Amount annually paid for labor.............................. 35,000
Setts cards in mill......................................... 10
Lbs. scoured wool annually consumed......................... 200,000
Lbs. cotton warps     "      "     ......................... 75,000
Lbs. woolen dress goods annually manufactured............... 165,200
Lbs. woolen and cotton warp manufactured.................... 70,500
Tons freight annually handled............................... 762

WORKS OF THE HOPKINS & ALLEN MANUFACTURING CO.

# PISTOL MANUFACTORIES.

NORWICH, for many years, has been very largely interested in the manufacture of pistols ; and the making of these familiar and dangerous weapons has long been one of the chief industries of this city. A few years ago, it was said that more pistols were annually made in Norwich than in all the other pistol manufactories in the United States combined. As late as 1882 and 1883, when the trade began to fall off, from 45,000 to 50,000 pistols a month were the products of the several manufactories in the city. Owing to over-production, close competition and the decreased demand from foreign countries, the business in Norwich, as it has in many other places, has become less remunerative than formerly, especially on the cheap class of pistols, and several of the shops have stopped manufacturing, until times are better and prices more satisfactory. It is rumored that one of the large pistol shops now lying idle, will turn its attention to the manufacture of a new and improved patent gun, provided the works can be turned into a joint stock company.

## THE HOPKINS & ALLEN FIRE ARMS CO.,

whose extensive works on Franklin Street occupy nearly a whole square, is one of the largest concerns in this state engaged in this branch of industry, ranking third in importance to Colt's, at Hartford, and Winchester, at New Haven. They manufacture a superior class of pistol, and also a celebrated grade of shot guns and rifles, which find purchasers in all parts of the civilized world. The firm first commenced the manufacture of pistols in this city in 1868, and have successfully pursued the business from that date.

| | |
|---|---|
| Capital stock.... ............. ........... | ..$ 125,000 |
| Average number of hands employed....... | 175 |
| Amount annually paid for labor....... ........ | ....$ 120,000 |
| Value of yearly products....... .......... | ......$ 175,000 |
| Number of guns and rifles made in a year | 6,000 |
| Number of pistols made in a year ........ | 100,000 |

WORKS OF THE NORWICH BLEACHING, DYEING AND PRINTING COMPANY.

EAST MAIN STREET, NORWICH, CONN

## THOS. E. RYAN'S PISTOL MANUFACTORY,

on Franklin Street, of which Mr. Ryan is the sole proprietor, commenced business eleven years ago.

| | |
|---|---|
| Number of hands employed..................... | 45 |
| Amount annually paid for labor.......... | $ 20,000 |
| Number of pistols made in a year.... | 30,000 |

## BACON ARMS CO.

The manufacture of pistols was first commenced under the name of the above firm in 1858, by Thos. K. Bacon. A few years afterwards it was made a joint stock company, the business was enlarged, and for a long time did a successful business. For the last two or three years the company have given up the manufacture of pistols, and are making a breech-loading, single-barrel gun, with reduced help from what they previously employed.

| | |
|---|---|
| Capital stock........................ | $ 40,000 |
| Number of hands employed................... | 20 |
| Number of guns made in a year.............. | 2,400 |
| Amount annually paid for labor............. | $ 10,000 |

# MISCELLANEOUS INDUSTRIES.

## NORWICH BLEACHING, DYEING & PRINTING CO.

This mammoth establishment commenced bleaching and calendering in 1840, and has expanded its works from year to year, until at present, it has grown to be one of the largest, if not *the* largest concern in America, engaged in this particular industry. The works are located Greeneville, and cover over a vast area of ground.

| | |
|---|---|
| Capital stock........................ | 500,000 |
| Yards cotton goods annually turned off, about.............. | 50,000,000 |
| Number of hands employed................... | 350 |
| Amount annually paid for labor............. | $ 200,000 |

## NORWICH & WORCESTER CAR AND MACHINE SHOPS.

Norwich is the southern terminus of the Norwich & Worcester railroad, and the shops for repairs and making the rolling stock for the
road, are located in this city. The company manufacture locomotives,
passenger, freight and dirt cars, besides doing all their own repairs,
which make an important item in the number of men they employ, and
their annual disbursements.

Number of men employed................................... 175
Amount annually paid for labor..............................$ 120,000

## THE NORWICH LOCK MANUFACTURING CO.

is not only one of the largest among the miscellaneous industries of our
city, but one of the three largest concerns in the country engaged in the
manufacture of locks, padlocks, and builders' hardware. The works
have been in operation for fifteen years. The variety and patterns of
goods manufactured is something enormous, requiring a list of twelve
closely printed 8 x 12 pages, two columns to a page.

Capital stock...............................................$ 75,000
Amount annually paid for labor...........................$ 100,000
Number of hands employed................................. 275
Tons of freight handled per annum, about.................. 2,200

## CHELSEA PAPER MANUFACTURING CO.

This is another of the huge establishments that has long identified
Norwich as a large and important manufacturing centre. The works are
established at Greeneville, within the city limits, and commenced oper-
ations as long ago as 1835. It manufactures printing paper of an extra
quality, and for many years has supplied the Harper Brothers, of New
York, with paper for their many publications, including Harper's
Monthly, Harper's Weekly, Harper's Bazaar, etc.

Capital stock...............................................$ 200,000
Lbs. paper manufactured per annum.......................10,000,000
Amount annually paid for labor............................$ 120,000
Number of hands employed................................. 230
Tons of freight annually received at works................ 15,000

WORKS OF THE NORWICH LOCK MANUFACTURING COMPANY.

## THE RICHMOND STOVE CO.

This is another of our large industries, which has added much to the growth and prosperity of our city. The works were first started in 1867, by Apollos Richmond, of Brooklyn, Conn., who had long been identified with A. C. Barstow, of Providence, in the manufacture of stoves, furnaces, etc. The increased demands for the products of this manufactory from year to year, have necessitated the building of large additions from time to time, so that at present the works extend over a vast space of ground. The company manufacture first-class warm-air furnaces, steam heaters, ranges, parlor and cooking stoves, which are on sale in nearly every city of the Union.

Capital stock................................................$ 150,000
Amount paid for labor per annum............................$ 100,000
Number of hands employed...................................    150
Tons of iron, coal, etc., handled per annum................   5,000

## COLD SPRING IRON WORKS.

One of the oldest concerns in the state that has been engaged in the manufacture of iron, having been first started in 1845. The works are located at Thamesville, on the Thames river, a mile from the center of the city, and are easily accessible by water for the loading and unloading of the heavy material that the works receive and ship to different points. The plant is owned and managed by Mitchell Brothers, and the products are merchantable iron of various kinds.

Number of hands employed...................................    50
Amount paid annually for labor.............................$ 30,000
Tons scrap iron      "      consumed.......................  3,000
  "   coal           "      "    in furnaces...............  2,500
  "   fire-brick, sand, etc., annually consumed............   300
  "   merchantable iron      "    manufactured.............  2,200

## THE NORWICH NICKEL WORKS.

Gen. Wm. A. Aiken is the manager and sole proprietor  Factory on Chestnut Street, and do electro-plating in nickel, silver and gold. Also, manufactures nickel plated window display fixtures for exhibiting goods in stores.

Number of men employed ...                                   25

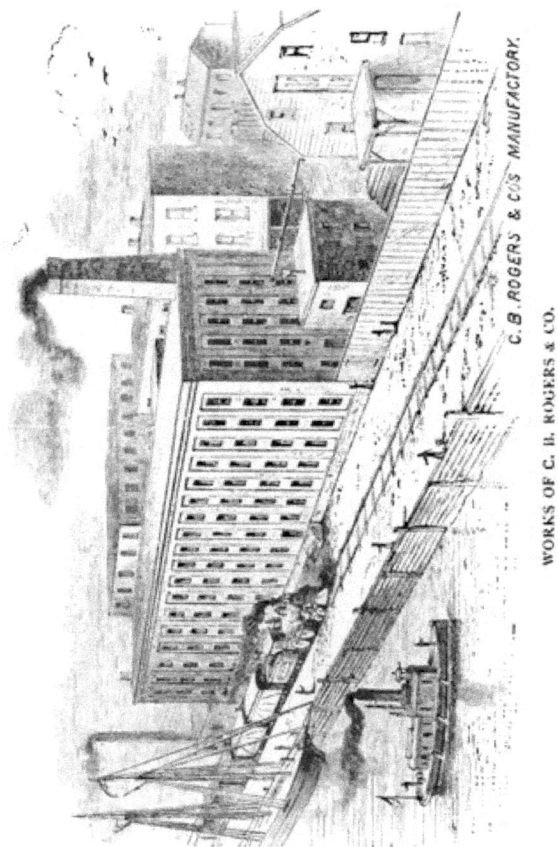

C. B. ROGERS & CO'S MANUFACTORY.

WORKS OF C. B. ROGERS & CO.

CLIFF STREET, NORWICH, CONN.

## C. B. ROGERS & CO.

### *Makers of Wood-Working Machinery.*

These works were first started by Caleb B. Rogers, in 1846, on a small scale, but gradually increased, so that in 1863 it was incorporated as a joint stock company. Their machinery finds sale not only in various sections of this country, but is exported to South America, Mexico, New Zealand, Australia, and various points of Europe.

| | |
|---|---:|
| Capital stock | $ 200,000 |
| Amount paid for labor per annum | $ 70,000 |
| Tons freight handled per annum | 1,200 |
| Number of hands employed | 125 |

## THAMES IRON WORKS,

are located in the immediate vicinity of the Cold Spring Iron Works, and are but a few hundred feet apart. A joint stock company, which was organized and commenced business in 1863. Its products are bar and spike iron.

| | | | |
|---|---|---|---:|
| Capital stock | | | $ 20,000 |
| Number of hands employed | | | 45 |
| Amount paid annually for labor | | | $ 30,000 |
| Tons coal | " | consumed in furnaces | 3,500 |
| " of iron | " | manufactured | 3,000 |

## ALLEN SPOOL AND PRINTING CO.

Their factory is on Franklin Street, and is managed by Edwin Allen, the inventor of the machinery. It is a joint stock company, and requires but a small capital. The work is mostly done by boys.

| | |
|---|---:|
| Capital stock | $ 15,000 |
| Amount paid annually for labor | $ 10,000 |
| Number of hands employed | 24 |
| Amount of products per annum, about | $ 30,000 |

## THE OSSAWAN MILLS CO.

The factory on East Broad Street is the largest one in the country that makes the manufacture of picture, shade and furniture cord a specialty. The labor is mostly performed by girls. Since the introduction of fine varieties of wire in the making of picture cord, the company consumes a ton a week of this article.

Capital stock.................. .............................$  20,000
Amount paid annually for labor.............................$   9,000
Number of hands employed............................. .............     40

## NORWICH CORK MANUFACTORY.

Previous to 1855, all the corks used in this country were imported from Spain and Portugal, where they were cut by hand.    In that year, the brothers, J. D. & W. R. Crocker, of Norwich, invented and perfected the first machine that was ever made for cutting corks by machinery.    This invention has been the means of working a revolution in the manufacture of corks all over the world, and in reducing the prices.    The Crocker machines are now not only in operation in several of our American cities, but also in Europe, where they have superseded the hand-labor process.    Barnes & Co., of this city, organized a company in 1856, and first put the machines in practical operation, importing the cork-wood bark from Spain and Portugal, the countries where it grows.    At present, the business is carried on in Norwich by Richard F. Goodwin, at his works on Franklin Street.

Number of machines in operation......................        8
Number of corks annually manufactured, about..............  10,000,000
Number of hands employed, mostly boys... .... ...........  .     10
Amount annually paid for labor.......... ...............$   4,000

## NORWICH BELT MANUFACTURING CO.

This is an important industry, that was commenced in Norwich in 1873, and has increased to one of large magnitude. The company make, in addition to belts, various kinds of goods for manufacturers' use, which find a large and ready sale all over the country.    They have an office and depots for the sale of their goods in New York, Philadelphia and Chicago.    Works are situated between Greeneville and Taftville.

Amount of products sold per annum.................. .. ....$  300,000
Tons of freight handled per annum.  ........................   1,500
Number of hides worked into belts per annum ................  15,000
Number of hands employed.... .... ............ ..     60
Amount annually paid for labor....................... .. .......$  30,000

## NORWICH MALT COMPANY.

A new industry that has recently been introduced in Norwich, and that has not fairly yet got in operation. It is a joint stock company, and obtained its charter a little over a year ago, in 1886, for making malt by a new process, which promises a handsome profit on the investment. Works located in the Elevator building, on Central wharf.

| | |
|---|---|
| Capital stock........................ .................. | $ 60,000 |
| Bushels of barley made into malt per annum..... ..... | 175,000 |
| Number of hands at present employed..... ............. | 10 |
| Yearly expenses including salaries .. ............. | 10,500 |

## C. H. DAVIS & CO'S PORK PACKING ESTABLISHMENT.

Works located on the Taftville road, above Greeneville. Products sold principally throughout New England.

| | |
|---|---|
| Number of hogs slaughtered and packed annually................ | 16,000 |
| "        " men employed........................................ | 12 |
| Amount paid for labor per annum............................... | $ 10,000 |

## CHELSEA FILE WORKS.

Commenced manufacturing and recutting files, in their present establishment near Franklin Square, in 1863. Their files are sold throughout New England, and the West.

| | |
|---|---|
| Number of men employed....... ... | 30 |
| Amount paid annually for labor....... | ...$ 12,000 |

## THE WM. H. PAGE WOOD TYPE CO.

These works have been in operation a number of years, and their celebrated wood type, which is made by machinery, is used in the majority of printing establishments throughout the country, and also to a large extent in South America and the West Indies. A new process of making wood type, very recently invented by one of the firm, will enable this company to more than double the present amount of business with the same number of hands now employed.

| | |
|---|---|
| Capital stock.................... .. | ...$ 10,000 |
| Number of hands employed........... | 40 |
| Amount of products per annum, about  . | ..$ 45,000 |
| Amount paid for labor per annum ... | . $ 18,000 |

## LESTER & WASLEY.

This firm manufacture envelope machinery, in their works on Franklin Street.

Number of hands employed............................ ..     12
Amount paid for labor per annum.. ...................$  12,000


## THE SIBLEY MACHINE CO.

This company manufacture paper machinery, paper engines, cotton and woolen machinery, etc.

Capital stock................. ... .................$  12,000
Number of hands employed........................... ......     40
Amount paid for labor per annum........................$  15,000
Amount of business done per annum...................$  140,000


## J. H. CRANSTON,

*Manufacturer Printing Presses.*

Works situated at Thamesville, and turning off a large number of printing presses annually, which are sold all over the country, and many exported abroad.    Commenced business in 1879.

Number of hands employed...... ............. .......     60
Amount annually paid for labor. .................. .............$  36,000
    "    of annual sales....................................$  95,000


## PAGE STEAM HEATING COMPANY.

A joint stock company whose works are located on the Greeneville road, a short distance from the business centre of the city.    Its celebrated steam heaters, which have gained a high reputation for doing satisfactory and effective work, are sold in the various states.    Col. W. C. Mowry, is treasurer and manager of the works.

Capital stock.... ............ .............................$  20,000
Number of hands employed................................     10
Amount annually paid for labor..............................$  10,000

FRANKLIN SQUARE, NORWICH, CONN.

## BENGAL CHUTNEY MANUFACTORY.

A recent industry which has been introduced in Norwich, and which promises to be of much importance in the future, its sales constantly increasing. Its factory for manufacturing located on Chestnut St.

Number of hands employed............................ ........ ...   12
Amount annually paid for labor... ......... ............. ....$  5,000

## THAMES KNITTING CO.

Manufactures stockinets. Works on Franklin Street.

Capital stock........................................... $  10,000
Machines run....................................................  25

## J. B. MERROW & SONS.

Manufacturers of crochet machines for finishing the edges of knit goods, occupy rooms in Myers & Bailey building, on Franklin Street.

## NORWICH HOSIERY CO.,

Manufacture cotton hosiery, and run 14 knitting machines. Occupy rooms in Myers & Bailey building, on Franklin Street.

The above three concerns employ about 30 hands, and pay out in the neighborhood of $15,000 per annum for labor.

## J. P. COLLINS & COMPANY.

*Manufacturers of Turbine Water Wheels and heavy Mill Machinery.*

Works on West Thames Street.

Number of men employed ............................. ............   20
Amount paid annually for labor.... .... ......       ...$  10,000
Tons weight material annually used... .... ........          200

3

## NORWICH IRON FOUNDRY,

*A. H. Vaughn & Sons, Proprietors.*

Established in 1854.

Number of men employed.................................... 35
Amount paid annually for labor.............................$ 20,000
Tons of iron consumed annually............................ 600

## A. W. PRENTICE & CO.,

*Manufacturers of Cotton Ropes, Cords and Twines.*

This is probably one of the oldest rope-walks in the state, having been established in the latter part of the eighteenth century. For many years it was known as " John Breed's Rope-walk," and did a large business in making heavy ropes and cordage.

Number of men employed.................................... 6
Amount paid annually for labor. ..........................$ 5,000

The above list, with the exception of one large mill in Greeneville, which declined to give any statistics to the Board of Trade, comprises all the manufactories in Norwich that are in active operation at the present time. It will be seen that there are in all, with the one exception, thirty-nine industries, or manufactories.

A. H. VAUGHN & SONS' FOUNDRY.

## Summary of the Norwich Manufactories.

| | No. of Hands Emp'd. | Amount Paid Labor. | No. of Spindles. | Yards Goods Manuf'd. | Lbs. Cotton Consumed Annually. | No. of Cards. | Lbs. of Wool Consumed Annually. | Tons Freight Handled. | No. of Guns and Pistols Made. | Lbs. of Paper Made. | No. of Corks Made. | Value Yearly Products. | No. of Hogs Slaug'd. | Bushels Malt Made. |
|---|---|---|---|---|---|---|---|---|---|---|---|---|---|---|
| 4 Cotton Mills | 2,800 | $ 810,000 | 184,000 | 34,500,000 | 8,850,000 | 37½ | | 15,000 | | | | $ | | |
| 4 Woolen Mills | 430 | 140,080 | | 2,600,000 | | 32½ | 1,200,020 | 4,512 | | | | | | |
| 3 Fire Arms Companys | 240 | 150,000 | | | | | | | 132,400 | | | | | |
| 1 Bleaching, Dy'g & P'g Co. | 350 | 200,000 | | 50,000,000 | | | | | | | | | | |
| 4 Machine Shops | 337 | 217,000 | | | | | | | | | | | | |
| 1 Lock Manufactory | 275 | 103,000 | | | | | | | | | | | | |
| 1 Paper Mill | 230 | 150,000 | | | | | | 2,800 | | 10,000,000 | | | | |
| 2 Stove Foundry | 150 | 100,000 | | | | | | 15,000 | | | | | | |
| 2 Iron Works | 95 | 66,000 | | | | | | 5,000 | | | | | | |
| 1 Spool and Printing Co | 25 | 16,000 | | | | | | 14,500 | | | | | | |
| 1 Picture Cord Factory | 40 | 9,000 | | | | | | | | | | | | |
| 1 Cork Factory | 10 | 4,000 | | | | | | | | | 10,000,000 | 300,000 | | |
| 1 Belt Factory | 66 | 30,000 | | | | | | | | | | | | |
| 1 Pork Packing Co | 18 | 10,000 | | | | | | 1,500 | | | | | 16,000 | |
| 1 File Works | 39 | 12,000 | | | | | | | | | | | | |
| 1 Wood Type Factory | 40 | 36,000 | | | | | | | | | | 45,000 | | |
| 1 Printing Press Factory | 60 | 8,000 | | | | | | | | | | 93,000 | | |
| 1 Bengal Chutney Co. | 18 | 16,000 | | | | | | | | | | | | |
| 1 Steam Heating Co | 30 | 15,000 | | | | | | | | | | | | |
| 3 Hosiery Companies | 30 | 10,000 | | | | | | | | | | | | |
| 1 Water Wheel Manufactory | 20 | 20,000 | | | | | | 200 | | | | | | |
| 1 Iron Foundry | 35 | 5,000 | | | | | | 600 | | | | | | |
| 1 Rope-Walk | 6 | 10,500 | | | | | | | | | | | | |
| 1 Malt Co | 10 | | | | | | | | | | | | | 175,000 |
| 1 Nickel Plating Works | 25 | | | | | | | | | | | | | |
| Totals | 5,344 | $2,110,500 | 184,000 | 87,100,000 | 8,850,000 | 32½ | 1,200,000 | 58,512 | 132,400 | 10,000,000 | 10,000,000 | $840,000 | 16,000 | 175,000 |

RESIDENCE OF W. A. SLATER, NORWICH, CONN.

# MANUFACTURING COMPANIES THAT ARE TRIBUTARY TO NORWICH.

NORWICH is really the center of the great bulk of the manufacturing interests of Eastern Connecticut. In the neighboring towns, and in many of the villages on the Norwich & Worcester and the New London Northern railroads, are a number of mills that are owned wholly or in part by Norwich capitalists, and depend upon Norwich for their mill supplies and banking privileges. That our city is greatly indebted to these outside interests for much of its wealth and prosperity, there is no denying. From these manufactories and their operatives our merchants derive a large trade, which has increased from year to year in the past, and promises to increase in the future. A large share of the freightage to and from these mills, passes through Norwich.

We give below a list of those from whom we have been able to get statistics.

## THE W. A. SLATER COTTON MILLS,

at Jewett City, nine miles from Norwich, is owned by Mr. Slater, who resides in this city. It has 16,000 spindles, consumes 2,280,000 pounds raw cotton annually, produces 6,500,000 yards colored cottons, employs 430 operatives, pays out $115,000 annually for labor, and handles about 3,200 tons freight.

## THE ASHLAND COMPANY,

in the same village, has a capital stock of $400,000, the great share of which is owned in Norwich. It has 25,000 spindles, consumes 830,000 pounds raw cotton, produces 1,250,000 yards cambric, twills etc., employs 350 operatives, and pays out $70,000 yearly for labor.

## THE GRISWOLD COTTON MILL,

in the town of Griswold, near the village of Voluntown, about twelve miles from Norwich, is owned by L. W. Carroll of this city, where he has his main office.

It has 11,000 spindles, consumes 800 bales of cotton yearly, produces 3,000,000 yards print cloths a year, employs 130 operatives, pays out $50,000 a year for help, and handles about 800 tons freight.

## BRIGGS MANUFACTURING CO.,

in Voluntown, has a capital of $100,000 and runs three mills with 15,000 spindles, consumes 900,000 pounds raw cotton, employs 200 operatives, pays out yearly for labor, $36,000.

A portion of the stock owned in Norwich.

## GLASGO YARN MILLS CO.

in the Town of Griswold, ten miles from Norwich, has a capital stock of $250,000—partly owned in this city. It employs 110 hands, to whom is paid $32,000 a year for labor. It manufactures fine cotton yarns and consumes 450,000 lbs. long staple cotton a year, and produces 340,000 lbs. fine yarns.

## ATTAWAUGAN COMPANY,

comprises three mills—the Attawaugan and Ballou Mills at Dayville, Conn., and the Pequot Mill at Montville, Conn., seven miles from Norwich. They have a capital stock of $600,000, the majority of which is owned in Norwich, where the main office is located. The company runs 46,000 spindles, consumes 5,000 bales raw cotton yearly, employs 800 operatives, and pay out $150,000 annually for labor. Freights handled 4,000 tons, and amount paid yearly for mill supplies $25,000. Main office in this city

## SAYLES & WASHBURN WOOLEN MILLS,

at Mechanicsville, on the Norwich and Worcester Railroad. Partly owned in Norwich. Employ 352 operatives, pay annually for labor $106,000. Setts cards in mill, 18 ; and manufactures 438,000 yards 6-4 cloth.

## WHITESTONE COMPANY.

Mills at East Killingly. Capital stock $200,000. Run 8000 spindles, employ 100 hands, consumes 900 bales raw cotton annually, pay-roll $25,000 yearly, handle 800 tons freight, and make 18,000,000 yards cotton cloth. Stock owned in Norwich.

## KIRK MILLS.

Situated at Central Village, eighteen miles from Norwich. The two mills run 11,000 spindles, employ 125 hands, consume 1,000 bales cotton, pay $30,000 annually for labor, and make 2,500,000 yards cotton cloth. Tons of freight handled, 1,000. The mills are owned and managed by the Leavens Brothers, of Norwich.

## BOZRAHVILLE MANUFACTURING COMPANY.

Located at Bozrahville, eight miles from Norwich. Capital stock $80,000, number of spindles 7944, employ 120 hands, pay annually for labor $32,000, manufactured during the past year 2,219,761 yards light sheetings and twills. Pounds cotton consumed, 476,487. Stock owned in Norwich.

## HALLVILLE MILLS.

Located in Preston, four miles from Norwich. Employ 175 hands, and consume 720,000 pounds wool annually. Make 865,000 yards flannels, and pay out for labor $60,000 a year. Handle 2,200 tons freight. The Hall Brothers, who own and manage the mills, live in Norwich, where they have their main office.

## PALMER BROTHERS,

Manufacturers of bed comfortables, being the largest concern in the world that make the manufacture of this class of goods a specialty. They have three mills : one each at Fitchville, Montville and Oakdale, which is in the town of Montville. The three mills are in the immediate vicinity, and but a few miles from Norwich, and are partly owned in this city.

### FITCHVILLE MILL.

Number of hands employed, 275 ; wages paid annually, $80,000 ; number of comfortables made in a year, 1,000,000 ; consumes 12,000,-000 yards calico and 6,000,000 lbs. cotton, and other material for filling in making the million comfortables.

### MONTVILLE MILL.

Employs 150 hands—its yearly pay-roll amounting to $50,000 ; makes 400,000 comfortables ; consumes 5,000,000 yds. calico and 2,500,000 lbs. cotton annually.

### OAKDALE MILL.

Employs 75 hands, and pays out $25,000 a year for labor ; makes 5,000,000 comfortables ; and consumes 5,000,000 yards calico, and 2,-500,000 lbs. cotton and other material for filling annually.

### SUM TOTAL OF THE THREE MILLS.

| | |
|---|---:|
| Number of hands employed | 500 |
| Wages paid annually | $ 155,000 |
| Comfortables made annually | 1,800,000 |
| Yards calico consumed annually | 21,000,000 |
| Lbs. cotton and other material consumed annually | 11,000,000 |

## NIANTIC WOOLEN MILLS.

At East Lyme, sixteen miles from Norwich. Manufactures ladies' dress goods and flannels. Employs 150 hands, and its yearly pay-roll amounts to $40,000. Runs 12 setts cards. The mills are owned and managed by A. P. Sturtevant and Son, of Norwich.

## WILLIMANTIC SILK COMPANY.

Located just across the Shetucket river, in Preston, about a quarter of a mile from Norwich center.   Manufactures silk ribbons.   Employs ninety hands, and pays out to its help $25,000 annually.   Its capital stock is $20,000, and consumes about 10,000 pounds raw silk a year. Was organized sixteen years ago.

## B. LUCAS & CO'S WOOLEN MILLS.

At Poquetannock, four miles from Norwich center.   Manufactures flannels and dress goods.   Employ 48 hands, and pay out $20,000 a year for wages.   Make 325,000 yards goods, and consume 90,000 pounds scoured wool annually.   Run four setts cards, and 28 113-inch looms. The concern is partly owned in Norwich.

## GLEN WOOLEN CO.

Located in Preston, about five miles from Norwich.   Number of hands employed, 35 ; has 2 setts of cards, and consumes 75,000 lbs. of wool annually ; pays its help $12,000.   Owned and managed by A. P. Sturtevant, of Norwich.

## R. G. HOOPER WOOLEN MILLS.

Located at Montville, seven miles from Norwich.   Manufactures fancy cassimeres ; employs 70 men, and pays for labor $30,000 a year ; has 4 setts cards, and makes 240,000 yards goods annually.

## L. M. HEERY & CO. WOOLEN MILLS.

Located in Lisbon, on the Shetucket river, a few rods from the Norwich boundary.   Make cassimeres ; employ 325 hands, and run 100 looms and 17 setts cards ; pay-roll amounts to $75,000 a year ; consumes 1,000,000 lbs. wool, and produces 500,000 yards 6-4 goods.

## ALLEN WOOLEN MILLS.

At Hanover, ten miles from Norwich.   Manufacture flannels, tweeds and cassimeres; run 6 sett cards, and 10 narrow and 27 broad looms.

## AMBROSE REYNOLDS MILLS.

At Blissville, in Lisbon, three miles from Norwich centre.   Manufactures cotton warp flannels and shoddy ; run 2 setts cards, 24 narrow looms and 1 shoddy picker.

## B. F. SCHOLFIELD MILL.

At Montville, about seven miles from Norwich.    Manufactures satinets.   Run one sett cards and four looms.

## CHARLES SCHOLFIELD MILL.

At Montville.   Manufactures woolen goods.   One sett cards.

## BEAVER BROOK MILL.

At Baltic, six miles from Norwich.   Manufactures flannels.   Run two setts cards, and twenty-two looms.

## J. B. SHANNON & CO'S MILL.

At Baltic.   Manufactures flannels.   Run three setts cards, and twenty-four looms.

# WEST INDIA TRADE.

COMMERCIAL relations between Norwich and the West Indies existed previous to the commencement of the present century, and have been kept up most of the time since, though not on a large scale. Many of the merchants of former days laid the foundations of handsome fortunes by exporting and importing live stock and various kinds of merchandise to and from these islands. The only house at present engaged in the trade is that of J. M. Huntington & Co., which was established in 1858. During the thirty years that the firm had vessels plying back and forth between the West Indies and Norwich, the amount of merchandise they have brought here, especially of molasses and sugar, would represent many millions of dollars, a great portion of which found purchasers in Eastern Connecticut. In the year 1887, the importations of the firm were :

| | |
|---|---|
| 4,105 hhds. molasses from Porto Rico, 322 tierces " " " | $174,000 |
| 10 puncheons bay rum from Porto Rico, 70 barrels " " " | 7,300 |
| 24 hhds. sugar " " | 1,673 |
| 1,902 bushels salt from Turk's Island | 1,050 |
| | $184,023 |

In addition to this, the firm brought from New Orleans by vessel 501 bbls. molasses, valued at $10,900 ; and exported to Porto Rico cooperage materials, provisions, etc., to the amount of $22,500.

---

# RAILROAD FREIGHTS.

---

THE Norwich & Worcester Railroad forwarded from Norwich, from Dec. 1st, 1886 to Dec. 1st, 1887, 234,583 tons of freight, and delivered at Norwich in the same time, 51,595 tons.

## TONNAGE OF THAMES RIVER.

THE freight of all kinds brought up to Norwich by steamers and sail vessels during the past year amounts to 330,000 tons, valued at $4,000,000.

One-fourth of this was landed at Allyn's Point, seven miles below the city, and the balance, about 250,000 tons, valued at $3,250,000, was brought to this port.

The number of steamers of the "Norwich Line" that discharged freights at Allyn's Point and at wharf in Norwich to be transported north by the Norwich & Worcester Railroad, was 185; and the number of sail vessels with coal, pig iron, steel billets, etc., landing at the same places for railroad transportation was 450. In addition to these, there were 569 steamers and sailing vessels that landed freights of lumber, brick, iron, coal and other merchandise at the wharves in Norwich for Norwich parties, making 1,204 sail vessels and steam vessels in all.

## COAL AND LUMBER.

THE facilities for shipping lumber and coal direct to the wharves in this city by sailing vessels or steamers, instead of transporting by rail, which would be much more expensive, makes Norwich a desirable market for purchasing the supplies. By careful estimates, it was found that in the immediate neighborhood of 60,000 tons of coal was handled in Norwich the past year, which does not include the very heavy amount handled at Allyn's Point, and transported by rail to Worcester and points beyond.

Of the lumber trade, it was found that about 15,000,000 feet was handled in Norwich the past twelve months.

# COTTON AND WOOL TRADE.

NORWICH being the center of a large manufacturing district, its sales of raw material that enter into the making of cloths and of manufacturers' supplies are consequently heavy. The dealers in cottons and wools report their sales the last year to have been 3,000,000 pounds wool, and 5,000,000 pounds cotton.

# MILL PRIVILEGES.

IT may be imagined by many after reading the statistics which we have given elsewhere of the large number of mills that are already in active operation in Norwich, that all the available water power has been utilized. But such is not the fact, as there are several fine privileges that are so centrally located near tide-water and railroad facilities, as to offer great inducements to manufacturers to locate upon. The tunnel privilege, so called, on the Quinnebaug river about a mile above Greeneville, is one of the best unoccupied privileges in New England. It has a 22 foot fall with a capacity of 1800 horse power, and can be developed at small cost. The Norwich & Worcester railroad adjoins it, and the Taftville station is but 1100 yards away. The privilege, with the ninety acres of land that goes with it, has been recently surveyed by the Shetucket Company, to whom it belongs, for the purpose of putting it in the market. The Falls Company have a desirable privilege located a short distance above their mill at the Falls village. It has a fall of fourteen feet, and a 200 horse power, and but a few hundred yards distant from the New London Northern railroad. Near the Totokett Mills, above Taftville, is another privilege with 13 foot fall, and dam already built. It has a capacity of 140 horse power the whole year, and 360 for part of the year.

# NORWICH POST OFFICE.

THE following statistics, showing the business done at the Norwich Post Office during the year ending December 31st, 1887, have been kindly furnished the Board of Trade by Postmaster Avery.

## RECEIPTS.

| | | |
|---|---:|---:|
| Received from stamps, envelopes, etc. | $26,747 98 | |
| " box rents | 1,471 50 | |
| " waste paper | 4 17 | |
| | | $28,223 65 |

## EXPENSES.

| | | |
|---|---:|---:|
| Post office | $ 5,906 22 | |
| Postmaster's salary | 2,700 00 | |
| Letter Carriers' expenses | 5,554 93 | |
| Mail Messenger | 332 50 | |
| | | $14,493 65 |
| Net income | | $13,730 00 |

## MONEY ORDER BUSINESS.

| | | |
|---|---:|---:|
| Balance on hand January 1st, 1887 | $ 304 90 | |
| Domestic money orders issued | 44,830 74 | |
| " " " fees | 359 13 | |
| Postal notes | 4,167 89 | |
| " fees | 75 39 | |
| International money orders | 7,886 30 | |
| " " " fees | 105 10 | |
| | | $57,729 45 |
| Domestic money orders paid | $33,362 42 | |
| Postal notes paid | 4,206 67 | |
| International money orders paid | 1,118 74 | |
| Amount repaid | 470 22 | |
| Amount remitted by draft | 18,231 75 | |
| Balance on hand December 31, 1887 | 339 65 | |
| | | $57,729 45 |

## REGISTRY DEPARTMENT.

| | | |
|---|---:|---:|
| Number of letters and packages registered | 3,236 | |
| " " " " received | 3,783 | |
| " " " " in transit | 4,310 | |
| | | 11,329 |

## LETTER CARRIERS' DEPARTMENT.

Carriers employed............................                                  7
Delivery trip daily ..........................                               22
Collection "   " ...............................                              24

Registered letters delivered.......  ...........          1,407
Letters delivered. .  ............................         540,192
Postal cards delivered....  ...................             70,582
Newspapers, packages, circulars, etc. delivered........   432,234
Letters collected...............................           366,319
Postal cards collected....  ...................             56,090
Newspapers, etc., collected....  .............  .........   41,513
                                                          _____   1,518,235

## BOX AND GENERAL DELIVERY.

Letters delivered.........................  ............   506,142
Postal cards........ .........................             70,720
Newspapers, packages, etc........................         112,305
                                                          _____    692,167

## MAILING DEPARTMENT.

Letters mailed...  ....  ...............  ...  .........  1,160,334
Postal cards mailed.....  .......................         150,307
Circulars, newspapers, packages, etc....  ......  .........   696,870
                                                          _____  2,007,511

## GENERAL BUSINESS.

Total receipts from postage account....  ..............  ..$25,223 05
Balance on hand, money order account, January 1st, 1887...     304 90
Total receipts from money orders, etc.................      57,424 55
                                                                      $82,953 10

Total expenses Post Office......  .................  ....$14,493 65
Net income to department postage account....  ..........  ...   43,730 00
Total money orders paid...  ...........................      39,158 05
Total money orders remitted by draft.....................      15,231 75
Balance on hand Dec. 31, 1887......................            339 65
                                                                      $82,953 10


The Post Office receipts for the past year have been $3,000 larger than
any previous year.

## NORWICH NATIONAL BANKS.

| Name of Bank. | Organized. | Original Capital. | Present Capital. | Surplus. | President. | Cashier. |
|---|---|---|---|---|---|---|
| Norwich | 1796 | $ 150,000 | $ 220,000 | $ 15,000 | Charles C. Johnson. | Stephen B. Meech. |
| Thames | 1825 | 200,000 | 1,000,000 | 350,000 | Franklin Nichols. | Edward N. Gibbs. |
| Merchants | 1833 | 200,000 | 100,000 | 10,000 | J. Hunt Smith. | Charles H. Phelps. |
| Uncas | 1842 | 100,000 | 200,000 | 40,000 | Edwin S. Ely. | Charles M. Tracy. |
| First | 1864 | 300,000 | 500,000 | 31,500 | L. W. Carroll. | Lewis A. Hyde. |
| Second | 1864 | 100,000 | 300,000 | 60,000 | Edward K. Thompson. | Ira L. Peck. |
| Totals | | $ 1,250,000 | $ 2,320,000 | $ 606,500 | | |

## NORWICH SAVINGS BANKS.

| Name of Bank. | Organized. | Deposits. | Surplus. | Presidents. | Treasurer. | Assistant Treasurer. |
|---|---|---|---|---|---|---|
| Norwich | 1823 | $8,066,646.29 | $ 250,000 | Franklin Nichols. | Costello Lippitt. | Bartell W. Hyde. |
| Chelsea | 1838 | 3,704,719.00 | 70,000 | L. Blackstone. | Geo. D. Coit. | C. B. Chapman. |
| Dime | 1869 | 1,330,000.00 | 22,500 | E. K. Thompson. | J. Hunt Smith. | F. L. Woodward. |
| Totals | | $13,101,365.29 | $ 342,500 | | | |

SHETUCKET STREET, NORWICH, CONN.

# BANKS AND BANKING.

NORWICH is the banking centre of Eastern Connecticut, and carries a heavy capital to accommodate the many manufacturers and business men in this part of the state. It is safe to say that no city in New England of its size has better banking facilities founded on a sounder basis. The investments of the different banks are loaned on the safest securities, and depositors, as well as stockholders, have every reason to rest assured that their money and their interests are well protected. The following table, giving a list of the national banks, shows the amount of stock of each, and when first organized, together with the amount of capital stock, and the surplus on hand the 1st of January, 1888. It also gives the deposits and surplus of the savings banks on the same date. It will be seen that the six national banks have a capital of \$2,320,000.00, and a surplus of earnings amounting to \$606,700; while the three savings institutions have deposits amounting to \$13,101,365.39, and a surplus of \$342,500.00, all combined making the heavy total of \$15,421,365.39 of capital and deposits, and \$949,200.00 of surplus. The Norwich Savings Bank with its \$8,066,646.39 of deposits is one of the oldest savings institutions in New England, and, with one exception, has the heaviest amount of deposits of any similar institution in Connecticut.

Worcester, which claims at present, a population of about 100,000, has but seven national banks with an aggregate capital of \$2,250,000.00, and four savings banks, with an aggregate of \$19,000,000.00 of accumulated savings.

---

# STREET RAILWAYS.

STREET railways are not only a great luxury, but have become a public necessity in all of our cities. Norwich is not behind the spirit of the age in this respect, being well provided and accommodated with this convenient and pleasant mode of transportation. The street cars

4

commenced running in 1868, and the travel on them has gradually increased from year to year, and have proved such a convenience that it would be difficult to dispense with them.   One of the lines extends from Franklin Square to the upper end of Greeneville, a distance of 1¾ miles ; and another from Franklin Square through North Washington St. to Norwich Town and Bean Hill, a distance of 3½ miles.   From the latter line there is a branch that extends from Williams Park through Sachem Street to the Falls village, and from thence through Lafayette Street to North Washington Street, where it connects with the Norwich Town and Bean Hill route, a distance of about 1½ miles.   The line from Greeneville is being extended and the rails laid to Taftville, 2¼ miles, thus connecting that large and thriving village with our city.   It is expected that this extension will be completed, and the cars running early in the coming spring.

The cars run at stated intervals during the day, and until ten o'clock in the evening, thus being a great accommodation to merchants and others doing business in the city and living in the suburbs.

# CITY WATER SUPPLY.

No city in New England has a more abundant supply of good, wholesome water than Norwich.   The reservoir, which covers 66 acres, being 1⅛ miles long and an average width of 480 feet, is situated on high, elevated ground in the northerly part of the town, 2½ miles from Franklin Square, the centre of the city.   At this point the level of the overflow at the dam is 234 feet, and at tide water 253 feet, thus giving it a pressure or head that makes it of inestimable value as an auxiliary to our fire department in extinguishing fires.   The reservoir gets its supply from natural springs that flow into it from the surrounding hills, and a water shed of upwards of 400 acres.   It has a capacity of 350,000,000 gallons, and by a small outlay can be made to hold a much larger amount should future demands require ; but, at present, the supply is fully adequate to the wants of a city twice the size of Norwich.   The water from the reservoir is conducted as far as the Soldiers' Monument, at the head of Williams Park—a distance of 1½ miles—in two mains :

FAIRVIEW RESERVOIR, CITY WATER WORKS, NORWICH, CONN.

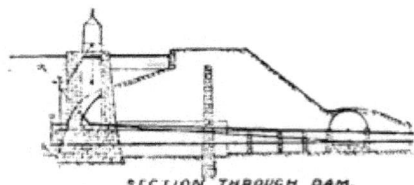

SECTION THROUGH DAM.

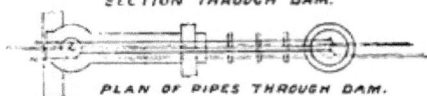

PLAN OF PIPES THROUGH DAM.

Note.—Meadowbrook i
through 24in. castiron
view Reservoir with a

### 1870.

Population        16000.
Cost of original works. $267669.12.
Distribution · Wrought iron cement lined.
10 inch. 43715 feet.
8     "     2216 ·
6      36841.5 ·
4   ·  19907
Less than 4in. 2363.5 · (Temporary.)
Total distribution 70705.5 feet.
Total length     79607.    "
No. Hydrants   85.
" Gates.       65.

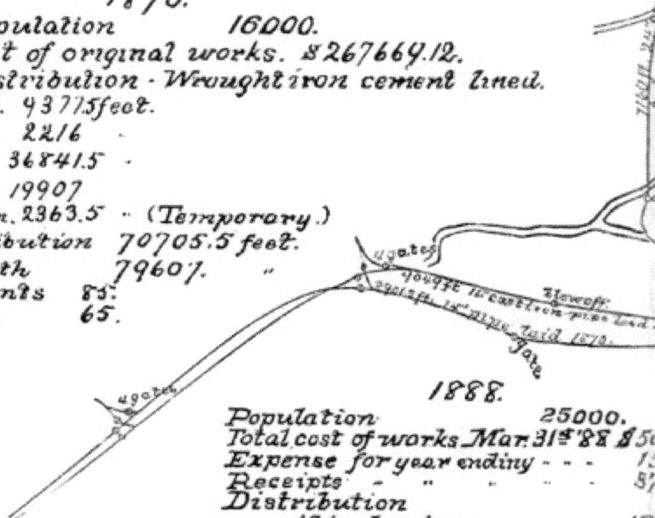

### 1888.

Population         25000.
Total cost of works Mar. 31ˢᵗ 88 $5
Expense for year ending - - -   1.
Receipts - " - "     8.
Distribution
     10 inch pipe.       19
      8    "    "
      6    "    "      8.
      4    "    "      4.
    Temporary small mains.   1
Total length of distribution   16
    "      "       18
Extensions and renewals. partly
Aver. estimated daily consumptio
Number of services      205
Length      ·      4832
No. of Hydrants      276
"    " Gates.      301.

### Plan of
# WATER SUPPLY
NORWICH CONN.
By C.F.Chandler C.E.

turned.
into Fair-
of 10 feet.

MEADOWBROOK RESERVOIR.
(Proposed)

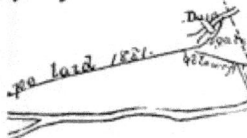

Dam

pe laid 1881.

Length            7000 Feet
Average Width   1250 Feet.
Area              260 Acres.
Capacity        1.000.000.000 Gallons.
Area of watershed      780 Acres.
Height of overflow   275 ft above meantide.

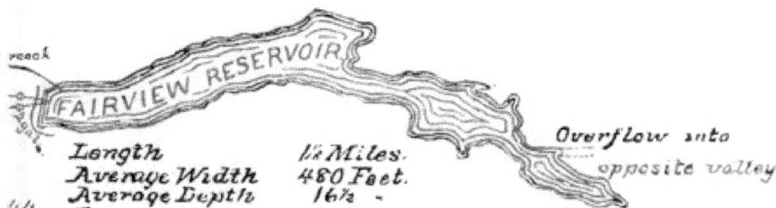

reach

FAIRVIEW RESERVOIR.

Overflow into
opposite valley

Length            1½ Miles.
Average Width    480 Feet.
Average Depth    16½
44.     Area              66 Acres.
5.      Area of watershed  483  -
0       Capacity        333.500000 Gals.
et      Elevation of overflow   240 ft above meantide.

Works designed by J. T. Fanning.
  "      owned by City.
Pressure in business portion 90 lbs.

on.
000 Gals.

one 16-inch and one 14-inch.    From this point water is distributed
through smaller pipes to all parts of the city, including Greeneville,
Laurel Hill, Thamesville and the Falls village.    At the present time
the water is supplied to 3,277 families, 815 offices and stores, 259 livery
and private stables, 318 garden hydrants and hose, 287 public fire hydrants, 20 fire cisterns, 16 school-houses, 22 fountains, 41 steam engines, 62 manufactories, 230 street front sprinklers, 45 saloons, 26
markets, 25 green-houses and graperies, 9 fire engine houses, and for a
large number of other purposes.    The amount received for water rates
for the year ending March 31st, 1887, was $31,897.02, and the sums
paid for keeping the works in repair, and for salaries and various expenses, amounted to $10,231.11, leaving a balance of $21,665.91 due
the city.    The total length of pipes now laid in the streets, including
the mains, is 188,666 feet, or a trifle less than 36 miles.

The distribution of 287 fire hydrants throughout the streets of the city,
and the pressure of a 250-feet head, makes the city almost safe against
a fire of any magnitude.    With such a force of water from a fountain
head of such large capacity, in connection with our efficient fire department, Norwich virtually insures itself against the devouring element.
Hose attached to one of the hydrants will easily throw a stream over
the highest buildings in the city.    The first public test of the fire hydrants was made in 1869, when under a 220-feet head, water was forced
through 200 feet of 2½-inch hose, with a 1½-inch nozzle, vertically, to
a height of 140 feet.    The whole cost of the water works up to the present time is about $600,000.

## SEWERS AND SEWERAGE.

It is difficult for any city or town to obtain good sewerage where it
is built on land that has an almost level surface.    In such localities
sewers may be, and are constructed, and if they do their work at all,
they do it sluggishly, and to little or no purpose.    Water will not flow
naturally  unless  moved  by  the  impetus  of  a  downward  tendency.

Many of our New England, as well as our Western cities, suffer from having been built on plain lands, where it is impossible to get good drainage, and, in consequence, are visited periodically with fevers, epidemics and contagious diseases. All of the great scientists of the present day, and those among the medical fraternity who have made the origin of various diseases and epidemics a special study, unite in affirming that a large majority, even if not all epidemics and scourges which sweep off its victims by the hundreds and thousands—often designated as "visitations of God,"—are attributable to the want of sewerage, or to imperfect sewerage. As an instance in support of this conclusion, the case of Memphis, Tennessee, is referred to, which was almost depopulated a few years ago by yellow fever. Here, on account of the even surface of the land on which Memphis is built, no public or private sewerage had ever been attempted; but when the dreaded scourge had almost wasted itself for the want of more victims to feed upon, the remnant of inhabitants awoke from their lethargy, and at an enormous expense and debt to the city, constructed sewers, with artificial flowage, which have seemingly had the effect of averting a repetition of the epidemic.

Happily, Norwich is so situated that it needs no artificial means to force running water through its sewers, or to wash its streets and gutters like Paris, and many cities which could be mentioned. Nature takes this work upon herself in our city, and often, after heavy rains and freshets, does it too lavishly. The streets lined with beautiful residences, ware-houses and public buildings, rising one above another, are built on lands that rise abruptly from the rivers' banks that almost enclose the city, thus giving a natural and almost effective drainage. In connection with what nature has done in this respect, Norwich has built within a few years 9½ miles of sewers, at an expense of $160,-000.00, through its principal streets, which empty themselves in a rapid current into the river. Vital statistics testify that there is no city in New England more healthy than Norwich, or one that is more free of epidemics of every kind, malaria, fevers or fever and ague.

Three years ago, 5,111 feet (a trifle less than a mile) of sewers were built in the streets of Greeneville, at an expense of $30,552.64, thus making that thrifty manufacturing suburb of the city a healthy, as well as a pleasant place of residence.

ST. PATRICK'S ROMAN CATHOLIC CHURCH, NORWICH, CONN.

FIRST BAPTIST CHURCH.

# CHURCHES.

NORWICH is well represented in churches, which embrace all well known denominations and societies. The buildings are so located as to be convenient to all parts of the city, and to cover the entire population, rich and poor, with the benign influences growing out of the organizations. In all of the churches there are well-organized societies for Christian work among the poor, in attending the sick, feeding the hungry, and for the purposes of extending a hospitable hand to strangers, thereby exerting a great influence for good. By the list given below, it will be seen that three of the churches were organized long before the commencement of the present century—the Norwich Town Congregational Church being the oldest, dating back to 1660.

The following list embraces all the church organizations, all of which possess comfortable buildings for holding services, several of which are handsome architectural structures, and ornaments to the city.

| | | | |
|---|---|---|---|
| First Congregational Church, Norwich Town, | | Organized 1660 |
| Broadway    "          " | 89 Broadway, . | " | 1852 |
| Second      "          " | 63 Church Street. . | | 1760 |
| Park        " | 283 Broadway. . | | 1874 |
| Fourth, | Greeneville. | |
| Taftville   " | Taftville. . . | | 1867 |
| Christ Church (Episcopal), | 78 Washington Street. . | | 1746 |
| Trinity   "      " | Church Street, | |
| St. Andrew's Ch. | Greeneville, . . | |
| Grace Chapel    " | Yantic. . . | |
| Central    M. E. Church, | 57 Main Street. | " | 1859 |
| East Main St.   "     " | 315  "    " | | 1853 |
| Sachem St.   " | 49 Sachem Street, | |
| First        " | Bean Hill, . . | |
| Greeneville.  "     " | Greeneville. . | |
| First       Baptist Church, | 239 West Main Street. | | 1800 |
| Central      "     " | 43 Broadway. | | 1840 |
| Third        "     " | Greeneville, . | | 1840 |
| Mount Calvary  "    " (col'd) | 49 High Street. | | 1871 |
| Universalist Church. | 298 Main Street. . | |
| German Lutheran Church, | 169 Franklin Street. | |
| A. M. E. Zion's Church (col'd) 362 | "        " | |
| St. Patrick's   R. C. Church, 205 Broadway. | | |
| Sacred Heart    " | Taftville, | |
| St. Joseph's    " | Occum, . . | |
| St. Mary's    " | North Main Street. | |

BROADWAY CONGREGATIONAL CHURCH, NORWICH, CONN.

PARK CONGREGATIONAL CHURCH, NORWICH, CONN

FIRST CONGREGATIONAL CHURCH.

SECOND CONGREGATIONAL CHURCH.

Making, in all, of different denominations :

| | |
|---|---:|
| Congregational, | 6 |
| Methodist Episcopal, | 5 |
| Episcopal, | 4 |
| Baptist, | 4 |
| Roman Catholic, | 4 |
| Universalist, | 1 |
| German Lutheran. | 1 |
| A. M. E. Zion's. | 1 |
| | 26 |

In addition to the above, is the Buckingham Chapel, 140 Boswell Avenue, connected with the Broadway Congregational Church, a neat and handsome structure, the gift of Governor William A. Buckingham ; and Trinity Church Chapel on Mt. Pleasant Street, connected with Trinity Church.

## PUBLIC LIBRARIES.

THE Otis Library, at the corner of Church Street and Broadway, was erected and endowed with a liberal fund for the purchase of new books by the late Joseph Otis, in 1858.    It contains at present about 15,000 carefully selected volumes, besides having on its tables about 50 American and foreign magazines and reviews.    All of the new and popular books are purchased as fast as issued from the press.    For the use of the books and periodicals a moderate sum is charged.

The library is open from 10 A. M. to 8 P. M. every day in the week, except Sundays, and its quiet alcoves are a pleasant retreat for those who have leisure hours for reading and looking over books of reference.

The library building is already too small to accommodate the rapidly-increasing number of books, and the indications are that in a short time it will be enlarged to double its present size.    It has a fund of about $20,000, the income of which is devoted exclusively to the purchase of new books.

OTIS LIBRARY.

The Peck Library, in the new Slater Memorial Hall, was designed by its donor, Mrs. General William Williams, more particularly for the benefit of the scholars of the Norwich Free Academy; but on certain days of the week it is open to the public, though none of the books are allowed to be taken from the building. It contains about 6,000 volumes, and has a fund of $10,000.

## YOUNG MEN'S CHRISTIAN ASSOCIATION.

The philanthropic and Christian organizations under the above name are rapidly becoming factors in the business and social life of our cities. There are over one thousand in the United States alone, and last year (1887) the benevolent contributions to these associations amounted to upwards of two millions of dollars. Six millions of dollars are already invested in association property, and the buildings recently erected are among the beautiful and attractive edifices of modern times, a practical demonstration of the value of their work.

The aim of the organization is "the improvement of the three-sided nature of young men,"—physical, mental and moral—commends itself to business men, in that, when demonstrated, better service is secured, and the moral tone of a city is made higher and more intellectual.

The organization in Norwich from the start, April, 1885, has had the warmest sympathy and support of the business men of the city. The rooms —ten in number—are located conveniently on a principal street, and are in arrangement and furnishing second to none in the state. The association, from the first, has been popular with young men—the average daily attendance being upwards of one hundred and fifty. The educational classes are of the best, the gymnasium is popular, and the religious services largely attended. Yet the organization has by no means struck twelve, and the ambition of the managers and friends of the association is looking forward to the day when, like similar institutions of other cities, they shall have a building of their own, adapted to their large and varied work. Strong encouragement has been given for the erection of such a building, the cost of which will probably exceed $50,000.

# DISTANCES BETWEEN NORWICH AND IMPORTANT RAILROAD CENTRES.

| | | |
|---|---|---|
| NORWICH from Boston, | 95 | miles. |
| " " Worcester, | 59 | " |
| " " Springfield, | 67 | |
| " " Hartford, | 48 | " |
| " " New Haven, | 63½ | " |
| " " Bridgeport, | 81 | " |
| " " Willimantic, | 17 | |
| " " Palmer, | 52 | " |
| " " Putnam, | 33 | |
| " " Waterbury, | 81 | |
| " " Middletown, | 47 | |
| " " Providence, | 51½ | " |
| " " Meriden, . | 66 | " |
| " " New Britain, | 58 | " |
| " " Norwalk, | 95 | |
| " " New London, | 13½ | " |
| " " New York, . | 136½ | " |
| " " Albany, | 280 | " |
| " " Buffalo, | 559 | |
| " " Cleveland, | 717 | " |
| " " Cincinnati, | 744 | |
| " " Chicago, . | 1034 | |
| " " Philadelphia, | 224½ | " |
| " " Baltimore, | 323 | |
| " " Washington, | 363 | |
| " " Pittsburg, | 567 | |

# EDUCATIONAL FACILITIES OF NORWICH.

To those who are seeking a change of residence, in order that their children may have the advantages of schools of the highest order and excellence, no place in the country offers greater inducements than Norwich. From an early date the subject of education has been of great interest to its citizens, and this interest has increased from year to year, until it has developed a high grade of schools, and a school system that has but few, if any equals in the country. In 1850, or thereabouts, the change was made from the old school system to graded schools. The change was not all made in a year, or five years, but the work, backed up by those who had the future interests of Norwich at heart, was gradual, until every district had new and beautiful school buildings, with graded schools of the highest order.

The Central District has five handsome school buildings, with graded schools of which the Broadway School may be considered the high, or grammar school.

The West Chelsea District has four school buildings, all of which are graded.

The Norwich Town, Falls and Greeneville Districts have each a commodious school building, with graded schools.

In addition to these, there are ten school buildings in districts of the town outside of those above mentioned, making in all twenty-two school buildings in Norwich, all of which are handsomely built, and with ample room for the scholars, which are increasing in numbers from year to year. The Broadway school-house, together with the new addition recently built, which is of equal size of the original building, cost over $60,000.

The enumeration of scholars in town between the ages of four and sixteen years numbers 2,515; and the apportionment of public money to the several school districts for the support of the public schools for the year ending August 31st, 1887, was $25,872.38.

SCHOOL HOUSES, (TAFTVILLE), NORWICH, CONN.

BROADWAY SCHOOL-HOUSE—CENTRAL DISTRICT.

## THE NORWICH FREE ACADEMY.

WHICH is the crowning apex of our school system, was dedicated in
1856.   For this noble institution, Norwich is chiefly indebted to the long
and persevering efforts of Rev. Dr. John P. Gulliver, who first con-
ceived the idea of establishing an endowed school of this class, and who
secured the co operation and generous contributions of many of our
wealthy and most benevolent citizens in carrying out the project.  Funds
sufficient to erect the present handsome and commodious building, and
endow it with a fund sufficient to employ an able corps of teachers
were at last realized, and very soon the much-talked of Academy, which
was to be free to the rich and poor alike, became a reality.    What its
success as an educator has been during the last thirty odd years is ap-
parent from the high stand its many graduates have attained in the several professions, mercantile pursuits and the various walks of life.

During the past year (1887) the scholars attending the academy—
boys and girls—numbered 253, all of whom, with the few exceptions of
those living outside of the town, worked their way up from the primary
to the senior departments of the graded schools of Norwich.   All those
who wish to enjoy the privileges of the academy are obliged to pass
rigid examinations in arithmetic, geography, history, English grammar
and spelling before they can enter.   The time for completing an
academic course, and before the scholar can graduate and receive his
diploma, is four years.

There are two courses of study : the classical course, which gives a
thorough preparation for college ; and the general course, which pre-
pares for practical life, or for scientific and technical schools.  At the commencement of the second middle year, scholars choose between the two
courses, and are assigned to the course they prefer.

It was at first designed by the trustees of the institution that none but
those living in the limits of Norwich should be admitted to the academy, but as the school gained in excellence and reputation, the requests
of scholars from outside the borders for admittance became so frequent
and pressing, that it was at last decided to discard the rule originally
adhered to, and allow scholars from the neighboring towns, or elsewhere,
the same privilege as those living in town.   To these non-resident pu-
pils a tuition fee of $10 a term of three terms a year is charged, in ad-
dition to the $5 for incidentals.

NORWICH FREE ACADEMY.

No scholars of the academy have more distinguished themselves, or brought greater honor to the school, than the many representatives from the country towns of Eastern Connecticut. A warm invitation is extended to all young men and women of this class who desire to enjoy the advantages of the academy, especially to such as contemplate a college course, to correspond with the principal, Dr. Keep, with reference to entrance into the academy. The school, at present, contains no boarding house of its own, but good board may be obtained, at low rates, in excellent families residing not far distant from the school. Most of the scholars who come from out of town, and there are forty at present, remain in Norwich only from Monday morning to Friday afternoon, and pay for board for only four-and-a-half days. In some cases, out-of-town scholars club together, and board themselves, thus making their term expenses very light.

The productive funds, whose income supports the academy, amount to $153,056.00. In addition to this, the several funds for scholarship, the Peck Library fund, the cost of the building and grounds, furniture and philosophical apparatus, swells the amount contributed to the permanent support of the academy about $240,000.00 since its incorporation in 1854. The beautiful memorial building, presented the trustees of the academy by Wm. A. Slater, for educational purposes in connection with that institution, cost $160,000.00, which makes the total assets of the academy amount to $400,000.00.

## THE SLATER MEMORIAL BUILDING.

NORWICH may well feel proud of the large and elegant building recently completed and presented to the trustees of the Free Academy by William A. Slater, in memory of his father. It is 150 feet long by 68 feet wide, and has a round tower on the front rising to the height of 145 feet. The structure is of dark red brick and brown sand-stone, resting upon a base of Monson granite. The whole of the interior is faced with pressed brick and terra-cotta, and the wainscotings throughout are of polished gray marble, which give a rich and pleasant effect. The first floor contains a large, spacious hall designed to be used by the scholars of the Free Academy for graduating exercises, and also, for lectures, concerts, amateur theatricals, etc. In the rear are two small halls, separated from the main hall with sliding glass partitions, which

5

can be thrown open, making one grand hall capable of holding 1,100 people. The large space over the main hall, comprising the two upper stories, is to be devoted to a museum, which is designed to be one of the finest, as well as one of the largest in New England. It is 47 feet high, and its four sides are encircled by an 18-feet gallery. The museum will soon be stored with rare and interesting treasures of art, gathered from the old world. Through Mr. Slater's generosity, an agent is now abroad purchasing *replicas* of art, and also, plaster-cast reproductions of the master-pieces of the great Roman, Greek and Italian sculptors.

A portion of the second and third stories west of the large museum hall is occupied by the Peck Library, and two large and commodious rooms to be used in connection with the Free Academy for classes in drawing, painting, etc. The Peck Library room deserves a more than passing notice. It is large and spacious, with lofty arched ceilings of polished cherry, with book-cases, tables, chairs, etc., made of the same wood. A goodly space of one end of the room is occupied by a large and beautiful terra-cotta fire-place and mantel, built after the style of "yᵉ olden time," and such as will be found in the baronial castles of the old world.

In the vestibule of the main entrance of the memorial building is an elegant bronze tablet, about five feet high and three feet wide, bordered with a laurel wreath, on which is the following inscription :

### This Building,

DEDICATED TO THE EDUCATION OF THE YOUNG,

AND COMMEMORATIVE OF JOHN F. SLATER,

IS ERECTED BY HIS SON,

## WM. A. SLATER,

AND BY HIM PRESENTED TO THE

NORWICH FREE ACADEMY,

IN GRATEFUL RECOGNITION

OF ADVANTAGES THERE ENJOYED.

# RAILROADS.

—

Norwich has two railroads, the Norwich & Worcester and the New London Northern. The former, of which Norwich is the southern terminus, is one of the oldest of the first two or three railroads that were built in this country, having been chartered as long ago as 1832. Since its completion, no road in the country has been more ably or carefully managed, or more free from accidents or mishaps arising from negligence, or incompetency. This road was leased to the Boston, Hartford and Erie R. R. Co. in 1869, and the lease assumed by its successor, the New York and New England R. R. Co., in 1885.

Between Norwich and Worcester, there are five regular trains that run daily each way, Sundays excepted. The steamboat trains that leave Norwich at 4:45 A. M., with passengers from the New York steamers that land at New London, connect at Putnam with trains for Boston, and the trains that leave Worcester at 7:40 P. M., and from Boston at 6:30 P. M. with passengers for New York and way stations, also connect at Putnam.

The New London Northern railroad, which passes through Norwich, runs seven daily trains, Sundays excepted, between different points on the road. Its northern terminus is Brattleboro, Vermont. Connections are made at Willimantic for Hartford, Middletown and New York, and at Palmer with the Boston & Albany and Ware River roads, for all points west and north. A late daily train from Brattleboro connects at New London with the Norwich line of steamers for New York, every evening, Sundays excepted.

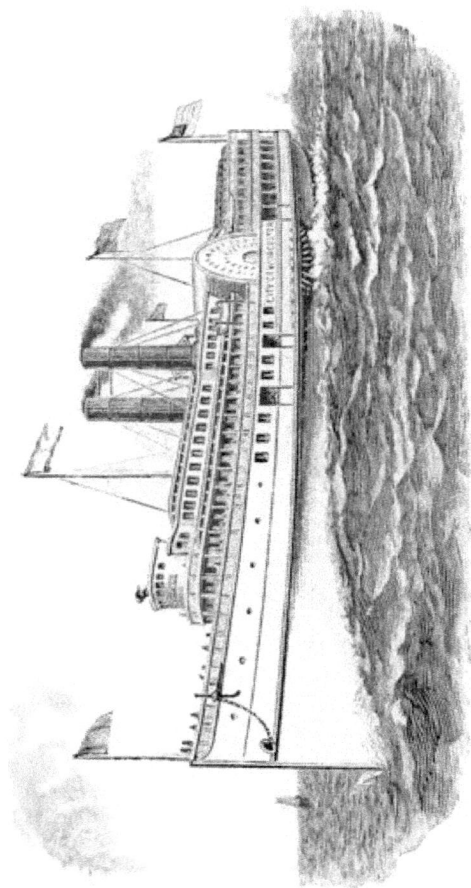

"CITY OF WORCESTER," OF THE "NORWICH LINE."

# STEAMERS FOR NEW YORK.

## THE "NORWICH LINE."

THE "Norwich Line" of steamers for New York is one of the oldest, safest and most popular routes that connect the great metropolis with New England. It is a daily passenger and freight line, and is controlled and operated by the New York and New England Railroad, the connections with which bring passengers from Boston and Worcester and intermediate points, and from the Boston & Albany, Worcester & Nashua, and New London Northern railroads. The line consists of five large, iron steamers, namely : the "City of Worcester," "City of New York," "City of Boston," "City of Lawrence," and "City of Norwich." The first three land and receive passengers at New London, and the two latter, the "City of Lawrence," and "City of Norwich," which carry freight principally, make Norwich their terminus on this end of the line. The "City of Worcester," which has recently been built, is one of the largest and most elegant steamers that plough the waters of the Sound. She is 340 feet long, 80 feet wide, and is built for strength, as well as elegance.

Persons traveling by the "Norwich Line" arrive at Pier 40, North River, at an early hour in the morning, in time to take all the early trains South and West by crossing the Pennsylvania Railroad Ferry, whose pier joins that of the "Norwich Line." The Norwich steamers leave New York daily, Sundays excepted, at 5 P. M. in the summer, and 4:30 P. M. in the winter.

In addition to the above steamers, there is a propeller line for carrying freight, that makes regular trips between Norwich and New York.

During the summer season, two lines of steamers run daily between Norwich and the summer resorts on Long Island Sound. Persons leaving Norwich in the morning by one of these steamers can spend the day, or a good share of it, at either Watch Hill, Block Island, Mystic Island, Fort Griswold or Pequot House, and return to their homes by six or seven o'clock in the afternoon.

# THE CITY HALL.

This building, which was erected fifteen years ago, is one of the hand-somest public edifices in the state, and of which the citizens are justly proud. It is built of Philadelphia pressed brick of the finest quality, with basement, lintels, window trimmings, etc., of faced granite. In addition to the city offices, which comprise the Council Chamber, May-or's office, Chief Engineer of the Fire Department's office, City Water Works, City Collector's and Treasurer's offices, are the Superior Court rooms, the Police Court rooms, the Town Hall for public meetings, the Judge of Probate, Town Clerk and Treasurer's offices, Selectmen's rooms and Police Head-quarters with twenty cells for criminals and of-fenders, offices for the Clerk of Courts New London County, and the County Commissioners. The building cost $360,000, and is an orna-ment to the city.

# POLICE DEPARTMENT.

NORWICH is well protected by its police force, which consists of eighteen efficient men, including its staff officers. In addition to this number, there are six special policemen, appointed by the Board of Common Council, to act in case of emergency. Within a short time three signal boxes: one on the corner of Franklin Square and Franklin Street; one at the West Side, corner of Thames and West Main Streets; and one at Greeneville, have been connected with police head-quarters, and give good satisfaction. By the telephone communication connected with these signal boxes, the officer in charge of the head-quarters can communicate with patrolmen in different parts of the city, day or night, at a moment's notice. It also enables patrolmen to send electric calls for help whenever occasion requires. The scarcity of burglaries, street brawls and thieving attest the efficiency of this department. Its cost to the city is about $17,000 per annum.

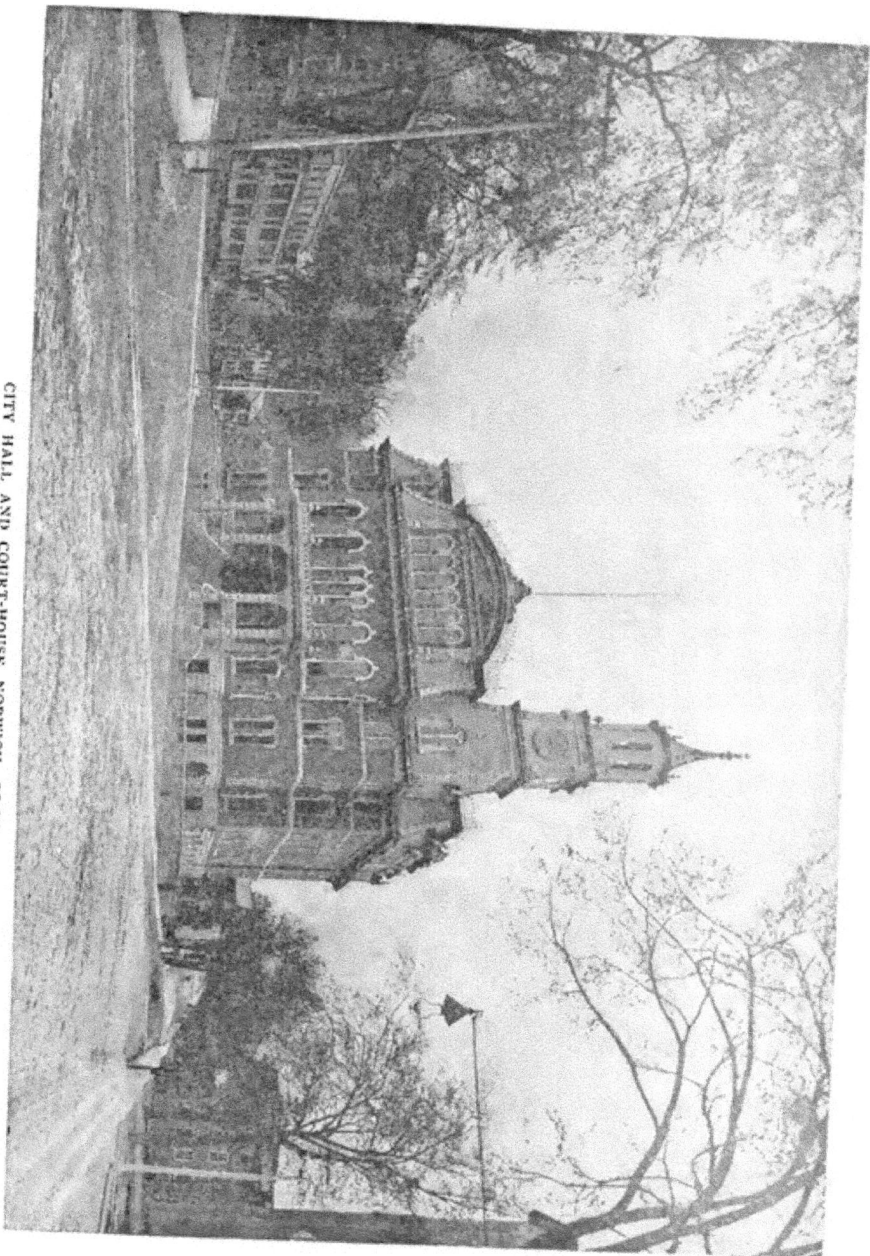

CITY HALL AND COURT-HOUSE, NORWICH, CONN.

# FIRE DEPARTMENT.

—

THE city has three steam fire engines, two hook and ladder companies, seven hose companies and nine engine houses. Twenty-three fire alarm boxes are located so as to be convenient to residents in all parts of the city. The department has 300 officers and men, 240 of whom are under pay for their services. Six thousand feet of hose are kept constantly on hand to be used in connection with the steam fire engines and the 287 fire hydrants that are located at available points throughout the city. As has been stated on another page, these hydrants are fed from the city reservoir, and have a pressure that throws a stream over the highest buildings, thus almost effectually protecting the city against a fire of any magnitude. The very few fires that have occurred during the last several years, and the small loss that has resulted from the same, attest the thorough and skillful manner in which fires are handled by the department and its efficient chief. The latter popular officer makes it his business to visit and personally inspect at intervals during the year all of the manufactories and buildings throughout the city to see that they are guarded from fires, either by accident, or from the improper construction of chimneys, flues and smoke pipes. The chief of the Boston fire department, who makes a specialty of recording all the fires, and their origin, throughout the country, recently stated that Norwich, according to its size, suffered the least from fires and the loss attending the same of any city in New England. The cost of the fire department to the city the past year was a trifle less than $10,000.

———

# LIGHTS.

NORWICH is well provided with light, both from gas and electricity. The use of gas, of course, predominates, and is supplied at reasonable rates. There are fifteen miles of gas pipes, which are not only laid in all the streets of the city, but extend out into the suburban villages. The electric light, which is supplied from the Thomson-Houston system, has lately been introduced into the city, and lights many of the business streets and principal stores. The gas company have a capital stock of $125,000, and the electric light company of $25,000.

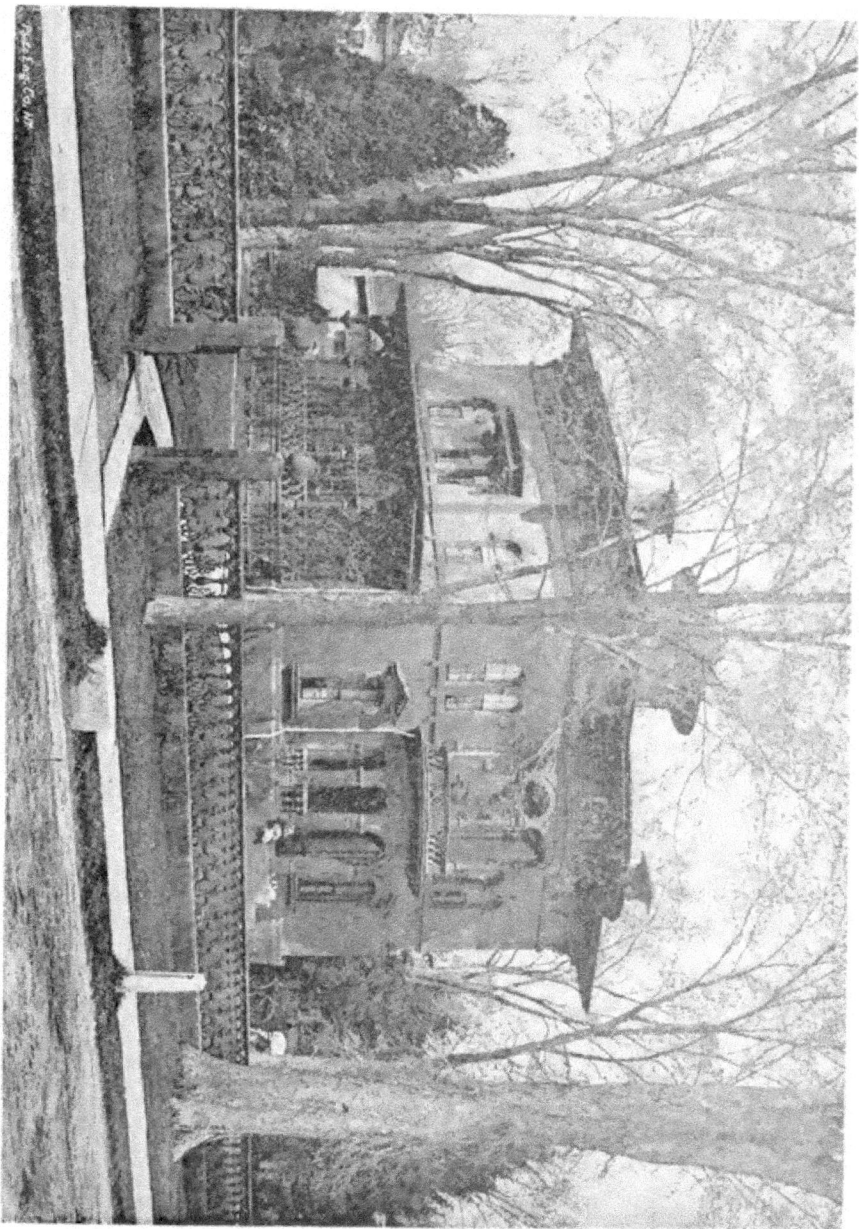

RESIDENCE OF HON. HENRY BILL, NORWICH, CONN.

# NORWICH AS A PLACE OF RESIDENCE.

So much of our space has been devoted to statistical information of the manufacturing and business interests of our city, it may be inferred by many who are strangers to the place that Norwich, like many manufacturing centres in New England, is not desirable as a place of residence. But such is not the fact. Probably no city in New England is more picturesquely situated, or more attractive in its varied beauties, than this same Norwich. Lying between sheltering hills, watered by the Thames, Shetucket, Yantic and Quinnebaug rivers, shaded from the heat of summer by lordly elms, oaks and maples, it excites the admiration and delight of all visitors, and has gained for itself the notoriety of being the most charming city in New England. It is the city and country combined. Stroll through Washington Street and Broadway, and view the beautiful private residences on either side of those charming thoroughfares. Where is their equal in outward elegance, or picturesque surroundings? Rest, for a moment in your stroll, at Williams Park, the *plaza* of the city, encircled, as it is, by fine elms and more of the beautiful residences which have made Norwich famous. A short distance to the east is a background of wooded hills ; and to the west, an open, undulating country, with vistas of forests, farm houses and streams of flowing water. Near by, and facing the park, is the handsome Slater Memorial building, the Free Academy and Park Church, which have been elsewhere mentioned. From the upper end of the Park, and near the fine Soldier's Monument, take the street that leads to Norwich Town, a mile or more distant, which was the original settlement long before there was a building where the city now stands. Here, perched upon a high, rocky cliff in the rear of the present church edifice, the first church was built by the early settlers—built high, and almost inaccessible, with a stockade around it to protect the building and the worshipers from the sudden onslaughts of the wily savages. It required a good amount of courage to attend church in those days, for there was likely to be danger lurking behind every rock and forest tree. The brave church-goers religiously carried their rifles with them, and during divine service armed sentinels were stationed outside to guard against sudden attacks.

In this old town lived the Huntingtons, the Hydes, the Fitches, the Clevelands, the Masons, the Tracys, and scores of others of honored memories, whose ashes have long since mingled with the dust.    Near the village green Mrs. Sigourney grew up from childhood amid the romantic scenery, the beauty of which she afterwards loved so dearly to recount in verse and prose.    Times have changed wonderfully since those days ; the public buildings have either been torn down, or changed into modern dwelling houses ; and with the exception of some very old gabled-roof shops, there is little to remind one of the past.    Standing upon the high rocks in the rear of the church, on a pleasant summer afternoon, one could imagine himself surveying the happy valley of Rasselas, so dreamy is the prevailing quietness, so gentle and noiseless the flow of the shining river as it winds and curves through the green meadows below.'

Returning to Williams Park by the northerly street, you pass the grand old mansion, once the residence of Gen. Jedediah Huntington a century ago, and where he entertained Washington in the dark days of the revolution.    Eastward of this, at the turn of the street southward, is a plain, unpretentious house, the birthplace of Lydia H. Sigourney, and where she passed her childhood days.  A mile or more south of this is pointed out the spot on which the house stood where Benedict Arnold was born, and passed his younger days.    The house was demolished many years ago, and nothing remains to remind one of this famous character—famous as a soldier, as well as a traitor,—but the old well and the curb that encloses it.

Arriving once more at Williams Park, turn down Sachem Street, you come to a place of great historical, as well as local interest, the grave of Uncas.    The last resting place of this warrior and chief of the Mohegan tribe is romantically situated in a small grove by the wayside, and is surrounded by the graves of many of his red descendants.    A plain, granite shaft, bearing the simple name UNCAS on the base, covers the ashes of him who was a monarch with his tribe, and whose authority extended over the country far and near.    The corner-stone of the monument was laid by President Jackson, in 1833 ; but the monument was not raised until 1842, when the ladies of Norwich completed the work

which had remained so long unfinished. Further down the street is a pretty, rural cottage, which will long be known and pointed out as having once been the home of Donald G. Mitchell, and where, under the *nom de plume* of "Ik Marvel," he wrote two of his best works—Reveries of a Bachelor, and Dream Life.

Still further west, taking either of the two short streets which lead in a southerly direction, you come to the Falls Village, which derives its name from what was once a romantic cascade, formed by the waters of the Yantic wildly plunging through a narrow, rocky channel from a height of about forty feet. In years gone by, "The Falls" was a famous resort for all strangers visiting the city, thousands being attracted to it by the wildness of the scenery, the rushing, roaring waters covered with white foam, together with the old legends connected with the locality, especially that of a band of Indians while being pursued by their enemies, jumping from the overhanging precipices into the boiling, seething waters below—a doubtful legend, to be sure, of Indian history, but of sufficient plausibility to give the place a weird and romantic interest. But what was known as "The Falls" of former days exists no longer in its original beauty and wildness, except it may be at times in the winter or spring, when the heavy rains and melting snows bring down vast bodies of water that come "tumbling and rumbling, and pouring and roaring like the waters of Lodore." The waters that once through all months of the year rushed madly down the rocky cascade, have been, in part, diverted through artificial channels to the great mills below, where they waste their strength in driving acres of machinery. The old rustic wooden bridge which spanned for so many years the roaring waterfall, and from which so many youths and lovers by moonlight and starlight have gazed upon the foaming waters beneath, has been removed by ruthless hands, and there is but little that now remains to connect the romances of the past with the business realities of the present.

Among the many beautiful drives and walks in and about Norwich, let the stranger not fail to visit Laurel Hill. Cross the fine iron bridge over the Shetucket from the eastern terminus of Water Street, and take the road that borders, and in many places nearly overhangs the river, for two or three miles, in the direction of Poquetannoc. No view on the Hudson is more romantic or charming. As you pass over Laurel Hill, its streets bordered by elegant houses, and surrounded by tasteful

and well-kept lawns, a beautiful panorama presents itself.    Far below
you the river Thames stretches its blue waters lazily towards Long Isl-
and Sound, while nearly beneath your feet, as it were, and within stone's
throw, lies the business part of the city.    It was but a few years ago
that Laurel Hill was a wild tract of hilly, mountainous land, covered
with laurels, rocks, wild cedars and brush ; a crooked cart path leading
over it, and scarcely an indication that it was ever under cultivation, or
even inhabited, if we may except a very old wooden farm house that
still stands in the background of the main avenue as a relict of the past.
Within a few years, this pleasant suburb has been constantly and largely
increasing, and promises eventually to rival in importance the older portion of the city as a place of residence.

Let the stranger, while in Norwich, be sure to visit Taftville, and see
the mammoth Ponemah Mills, which have been mentioned in a previous
part of this book.    The short journey will well repay the trouble.    It
is a pleasant drive to pass through the manufacturing suburb of Greeneville, with its long array of mills and store-houses that line the river's
banks.    About a mile above, he comes to Sachem's Plain.    Pause here
a moment.    In the open field yonder, on slightly elevated ground, is a
square block of granite, on the base of which is carved the name of
MIANTONOMOH, placed there to mark the spot where this celebrated
Indian chief was slain by his bitter enemy, Uncas.    A mile further, he
comes to Taftville, and the enormous mill springs up before him as if by
magic, and there seems to be no end to the vast pile of bright red brick
and countless windows that reach into the far distance, like giant's castles in childhood's dreams.    If there is time, go inside the mill, and
take a glance at the acres and acres of moving machinery, and hear the
hum, the whirr, and the rattle of wheels, and looms, and cards, and the
one hundred and twenty-five thousand spindles, operated by fifteen
hundred men, women and children.

Returning to the city, take the road to the left, and pass over Plain
Hill and Wawecus Hill, one of the most delightful drives in the state—
the high altitude enabling you to get a magnificent view of the country
far and near.    Here you see fine farm houses and farming lands border-
ing the highways, villages here and there nestling among the forest covered hills ; and occasionally you catch a glimpse of the river Thames as
it flows southward, and empties its waters into Long Island Sound.

DR. CASSIDY'S BLOCK, NORWICH, CONN.

WAUREGAN HOTEL, NORWICH, CONN.

# NORWICH, CONN.,

# BUSINESS DIRECTORY

## AND

# ADVERTISEMENTS.

# NORWICH SAVINGS SOCIETY,

## 24 SHETUCKET STREET,

### Incorporated May, 1824.

---

### OFFICERS:

**PRESIDENT,**
FRANKLIN NICHOLS.

**VICE PRESIDENTS,**

LUCIUS W. CARROLL,     JOHN A. MORGAN.
AMOS W. PRENTICE,     JOHN BREWSTER.

**DIRECTORS,**

JOHN MITCHELL,     LUCIUS BROWN,     GEORGE R. HYDE,
HEZEKIAH F. RUDD,     BELA P. LEARNED,     ASA BACKUS,
HENRY LARRABEE,     FRANK JOHNSON,     SIDNEY TURNER.

**SECRETARY AND TREASURER,**
COSTELLO LIPPITT.

**ATTORNEY,**
JEREMIAH HALSEY.

---

| Amount of Deposits January 1st, | | | | 1835, | $ 147,161.00 |
|---|---|---|---|---|---|
| " | " | " | " | 1845, | 264,305.00 |
| " | " | " | " | 1855, | 1,883,195.00 |
| " | " | " | " | 1865, | 4,202,191.00 |
| " | " | " | " | 1875, | 7,492,306.00 |
| " | " | " | " | 1876, | 7,750,466.00 |
| " | " | " | " | 1878, | 7,717,134.00 |
| " | " | " | " | 1879, | 7,382,768.00 |
| " | " | " | " | 1880, | 7,438,559.00 |
| " | " | " | " | 1881, | 7,552,799.00 |
| " | " | " | " | 1882, | 7,601,738.00 |
| " | " | " | " | 1883, | 7,801,362.00 |
| " | " | " | " | 1884, | 7,928,571.00 |
| " | " | " | " | 1885, | 8,088,825.00 |
| " | " | " | " | 1886, | 8,003,550.00 |
| " | " | " | " | 1887, | 8,279,529.00 |
| " | " | " | " | 1888, | 8,472,150.36 |

**Balance to credit of Surplus and Profit and Loss, Jan. 1, 1888, $401,959.44.**

# THE CHELSEA SAVINGS BANK.

## NORWICH, CONN.

### *Incorporated 1858.*

## Deposits, March 1st, 1888, $3,967,674.16

### DIVIDENDS, MARCH AND SEPTEMBER.

Deposits made the first business day of any month will draw interest from that date; all other deposits will draw interest from the first day of the next succeeding month.

### OFFICERS:

President, LORENZO BLACKSTONE.

**Vice Presidents:** HENRY BILL, JOHN T. WAIT, JAMES A. HOVEY.

**Directors:**

JOHN P. BARSTOW,  O. J. LAMB,  OLIVER E. AVERY.
EDWARD HARLAND,  GEORGE D. COIT,  HENRY H. GALLUP.
DAVID A. BILLINGS,  W. N. BLACKSTONE,  WM. A. SLATER.

**Counsel,** JEREMIAH HALSEY.  **Attorneys,** THAYER & THAYER.

**Secretary and Treasurer,** GEORGE D. COIT.

**Assistant Treasurer,** CHARLES E. CHAPMAN.

BANK HOURS—From 10 A. M. to 1 P. M., and from 2 to 3 P. M., except Saturday. Closed Saturday Afternoon.

# TheDimeSavingsBank

## OF NORWICH, CONN.

### *Organized September, 1869.*

## Deposits, March 1st, 1888, $1,350,833.69

Amounts received from Ten Cents to One Thousand Dollars. All deposits are placed on interest the first of every month.

### OFFICERS:

President, EDWARD K. THOMPSON.

**Vice Presidents:** HUGH H. OSGOOD, WILLIS R. AUSTIN.

**Directors:**

WM. C. OSGOOD,  W. R. BURNHAM,  GARDINER GREENE, JR.
F. J. LEAVENS,  J. HUNT SMITH,  GEORGE C. RAYMOND,
C. D. BROWNING.  E. G. BIDWELL,  J. W. CARPENTER.
  NICHOLAS TARRANT.

**Secretary and Treasurer,** J. HUNT SMITH.

**Assistant Treasurer,** FRANK L. WOODARD.

**Attorney,** GARDINER GREENE, JR.

# Thames National Bank

## 16 SHETUCKET STREET.

United States Depository.

### INCORPORATED 1825.

## Capital Stock, - $1,000,000.00

OFFICERS:

PRESIDENT.
FRANKLIN NICHOLS.

CASHIER.
EDWARD N. GIBBS.

DIRECTORS.

| | |
|---|---|
| FRANKLIN NICHOLS, | JOHN MITCHELL, |
| ALFRED A. YOUNG, | CHARLES BARD, |
| JAMES L. HUBBARD, | THOMAS D. SAYLES, |
| LORENZO BLACKSTONE, | EDWARD N. GIBBS, |
| WILLIAM G. JOHNSON, | WILLIAM A. SLATER, |
| HUGH H. OSGOOD. | HENRY H. GALLUP. |

## Discount Days, Tuesdays and Fridays.

BANK HOURS—From 10 A. M. to 1 P. M., and from 2 to 3 P. M., except Saturday.
Closed Saturday Afternoon.

# FIRST NATIONAL BANK,

### Richards Building, 87 Main Street.

*Organized 1864.*

CAPITAL STOCK,  -  -  $500,000

#### OFFICERS :

President, LUCIUS W. CARROLL.     Cashier, LEWIS A. HYDE.

**Directors :**

LUCIUS W. CARROLL,     CHARLES D. BROWNING,
JEREMIAH HALSEY,     FRANCIS L. LEAVENS,
AMOS W. PRENTICE,     CHARLES H. KENYON,
JOHN A. MORGAN,     R. N. PARISH.

## Discount Days, Mondays and Thursdays.

BANK HOURS—From 10 A. M. to 1 P. M., and from 2 to 3 P. M., except Saturday.
Closed Saturday Afternoon.

# SECOND NATIONAL BANK.

## CAPITAL, $300,000.00.

#### BOARD OF DIRECTORS.

E. R. THOMPSON     W. R. BURNHAM,
C. P. COGSWELL,     LYMAN GOULD.
W. R. AUSTIN.

## Mercantile and Corporate Accounts respectfully solicited.

# Norwich National Bank,

### Shetucket, cor. Main Street,

INCORPORATED 1796.

Capital Stock,  =  =  $220,000.

President, C. C. JOHNSON.     Cashier, S. B. MEECH.

## Discount Days, Tuesdays and Fridays.

6

# UNCAS NATIONAL BANK,

## 42 Shetucket Street.

Organized under the Free Banking Law of 1852. Incorporated by
General Act, 1855.

CAPITAL STOCK,        -        -        $200,000

### OFFICERS:

President, EDWIN S. ELY.        Cashier, CHAS. M. TRACY.

#### Directors:

| | |
|---|---|
| EDWIN S. ELY, | GEO. W. GOULD, |
| JAMES A. HOVEY, | NATHL. B. WILLIAMS, |
| JOHN T. WAIT, | ALDEN A. BAKER, |
| JOSEPH HUTCHINS, | EDWARD F. BURLESON, |
| | CHAS. M. TRACY. |

## Discount Days, Mondays and Thursdays.

BANK HOURS—From 10 A. M. to 1 P. M., and from 2 to 3 P. M., except Saturday.
Closed Saturday Afternoon.

# THE MERCHANTS NATIONAL BANK

## 71 MAIN STREET.

### INCORPORATED 1833.

## Capital Stock,  -  $100,000

### OFFICERS:

President, J. HUNT SMITH.        Cashier, CHARLES H. PHELPS.

#### Directors:

| | |
|---|---|
| WILLIAM C. OSGOOD, | WM. A. THOMPSON, |
| COSTELLO LIPPITT, | GEORGE F. BARD, |
| CHARLES F. SETCHEL, | JOHN D. BREWSTER, |
| CALVIN L. HARWOOD, | WM. H. FITCH, |
| J. HUNT SMITH. | CHAS. H. PHELPS. |

## Discount Days, Mondays and Thursdays.

BANK HOURS—From 10 A. M. to 1 P. M., and from 2 to 3 P. M., except Saturday.
Closed Saturday Afternoon.

ESTABLISHED 1840.

# New London County Mutual Fire Insurance Company,

## OF NORWICH, CONN..

Office, Richards Building, 91 Main St.

### Surplus, Jan. 1, 1888, $85,000.

*This old and reliable Company insures Dwelling Houses,
Churches, School-houses and their contents against loss
or damage by fire or lightning on
FAVORABLE TERMS.*

DIRECTORS:

E. F. PARKER,        DENISON B. COON,       E. L. OSGOOD,
P. St. M. ANDREWS,   E. L. GARDNER,         CHAS. J. WINTERS,
JOHN A. MORGAN,      C. H. OSGOOD,          JOHN T. POSWELL,
        J. F. WILLIAMS,                IRA L. PECK,

J. F. WILLIAMS, Sec'y.   IRA L. PECK, Treas.   E. F. PARKER, Prest.

# The Norwich Nickel Works,

### ELECTRO-PLATERS IN

# NICKEL, COPPER, BRASS, SILVER & GOLD.

ALL WORK GUARANTEED AGAINST FLAKING.

SPECIALTIES:

Fire Arms, Stove Castings, Steamboat and
Yacht Trimmings, Steam and Fire
Engine Work, Etc.

MANUFACTURERS OF

FINEST METAL DISPLAY FIXTURES

FOR STORE WINDOWS AND INTERIORS.

ADAPTED TO ALL TRADES.

TELEPHONE CONNECTION.

N. Y. SALES ROOMS,                    OFFICE AND FACTORY.
702 Broadway, New York.      51 Chestnut St., Norwich, Conn

# The Leader Envelope Machine,

Patented in the United States, Great Britain, France and Germany.

## MANUFACTURED BY

# LESTER & WASLEY,

## NORWICH, CONN., U. S. A.

*The Leader Machine will gum, fold, count and deliver in packages of twenty-five, ready for banding, at the rate of 100 envelopes per minute on Drug and Letter size.*

*These Envelope Machines are built in different sizes, viz: Drug, Letter, No. 9, 10, 11, 12 and 14. Estimates for other sizes, and any other information desired, will be cheerfully given on application.*

## ✦THE✦

# All Right Steam Heater.

Nearly **400** in use, and not one has ever given out, or cracked in use.

We are prepared to make estimates on all classes of Steam or Hot Water Heating, and guarantee satisfaction in all cases.

Circulars on application to

THE COMBINATION CO., No. 286 Franklin Street, Norwich, Conn.,

*or to WM. H. PAGE, Treasurer, same place.*

# J. B. Merrow & Sons,

MAKERS OF

## The Merrow Special Crochet Machine

For Finishing the Edges of Knit Goods, from the finest to the heaviest,

Is rapid, simple and satisfactory.

**18 and 20 White's Court,    -    Norwich, Conn.**

---

# NORWICH LOCK MFG. CO.,

MANUFACTURERS OF

# LOCKS, KNOBS,

AND

# BUILDERS' HARDWARE,

NORWICH, CONN.

---

## EXCLUSIVELY **HAND-CUT** FILES and RASPS

MANUFACTURED BY

# THE CHELSEA FILE WORKS

NORWICH, CONN.

## HORSE RASPS A SPECIALTY.

Patronize Home Industry by using the
"Chelsea" Files and Rasps.

---

LYMAN GOULD, President.                    R. W. PERKINS, Secretary.

# C. B. ROGERS & CO.,

Makers of the Latest Improved

# Wood-Working Machinery.

Principal Office and Manufactory, Norwich, Conn.

Incorporated 1863.                    Warerooms, 109 Liberty Street, New York

# The Hopkins & Allen Manufacturing Company,

MANUFACTURERS OF THE

Blue Jacket, XL, Army 44 and 45 Calibre,
Double Action and Automatic 38 and 32

# Revolvers, Shot Guns,

## AND RIFLES,

132 Franklin St.,  -  Norwich, Conn.

OFFICERS :

H. A. BRIGGS, Pres't.   JOHN E. WARNER, Sec'y.   C. W. HOPKINS, Treas.

Depot : Merwin, Hulbert & Co., 26 W. 23d St., New York.

---

# The Allen Spool & Printing Co.,

MANUFACTURERS AND PRINTERS OF

# Spools and
# Braid Rolls,

# COTTON ROLLS AND NOVELTIES,

132 Franklin St., Norwich, Conn.

# THE OSSAWAN MILLS CO.,

MANUFACTURERS OF

## Braided and Twisted Worsted, Silk, Cotton,

## AND WIRE CORDS.

### ALSO, THE CROWN SOLID BRAIDED CORDS,

NORWICH, CONN.

---

## RICHARD F. GOODWIN,

Successor to Goodwin & Parker. Manufacturer of

# MACHINE-CUT CORKS

## OF EVERY DESCRIPTION.

### SPECIALTIES--Cork Washers and Sliced Cork.

NORWICH, CONN.

---

# ANSEL CLARK,

MANUFACTURER OF THE

## Avery Low Pressure....

## ⊹ Improved Steam Heater.

This Heater is the most economical Steam Heater made or used.
It will heat a greater area, with less fuel, than others of greater capacity.
Testimonials and Price List furnished upon application.

ALSO,

## CONTRACTOR and BUILDER,

*Stone, Slate, Brick, Cement, Lime, Plaster, Hair, Fire Brick
and Clay, Beach Sand, Drain Pipe, Sheathing Paper, &c.,
AT WHOLESALE AND RETAIL.*

## Prompt attention to orders for MASON WORK of all kinds and SLATE ROOFING.

*Telephone.* 13 Water St., Norwich, Conn.

# A. T. CONVERSE,

### Office, Warehouse and Wharf, 23 Commerce St.,
### NORWICH, CONN.,

## Blast Furnace and Rolling Mill Products,

----INCLUDING----

Most Approved Brands of Foundry Pig Iron,

Special Grades of Puddled Bar Iron,

Galvanized and Black Sheet Iron,

Warranted Best Cast and Machinery Steel,

Rolled Iron Beams and Shapes for Structural
    Purposes,

Finished Shafting and Machinery for Transmis-
    sion of Power,

Etc., Etc.

---

# M. A. BARBER,

## Machinist and Engineer.

## All kinds of General Machine Work, Jobbing & Repairing.

SPECIALTIES—Cork Machinery, Laundry Machinery, and Steam
Engine Repairing.

Expert Mechanical and Indicator Work Solicited.

*No. 22 FERRY STREET,   -   -   NORWICH, CONN.*

---

## BREWSTER & BURNETT,

## STOVES, TIN WARE, AGRICULTURAL IMPLEMENTS,

### SEEDS, STOCKBRIDGE FERTILIZERS OF ALL KINDS.

Sole Agents for the " Good News " and " Magee " Ranges, and Magee Goods
OF ALL KINDS.

Tin Roofing and General Jobbing, Sheet Iron and Copper Workers.

*9 and 11 Water Street, Norwich, Conn.*

# NORWICH IRON FOUNDRY,

ESTABLISHED 1851.

### A. H. VAUGHN & SONS, Proprietors,

#### Nos. 11 to 25 Ferry Street, Norwich, Ct.,

# CASTINGS, OF EVERY DESCRIPTION,

## FURNISHED PROMPTLY.

## PATTERNS MADE TO ORDER.

---

# The Sibley Machine Company,

MANUFACTURERS OF

# Paper Making Machinery,

Paper Engines, Dusters; Rag, Rope and Paper Cutters; Roll Bars and Bed Plates.
Also, Cotton and Wool Machinery, Mill Gearing, Shafting, Pulleys and
Hangers, Reed and Bowen's Combined Expeller Shears and Punch.
L. B. West's American Pug Setter.

JOBBING OF ALL KINDS. CASTINGS AT SHORT NOTICE.

Agents for Hunt's Double-Acting Turbine Water Wheel.

*Telephone Connection.* *132 Franklin St., Norwich, Conn.*

---

# NORWICH BELT MANUFACTURING CO.,

TANNERS AND MANUFACTURERS OF

# Superior Oak Leather Belting

## Dealers in Saddlery and Mill Supplies.

### Rubber and Cotton Belting.

### Rubber, Cotton and Linen Hose,

### Rubber and Oiled Clothing.

### Leather of all kinds.

## Horse Blankets, Robes, Whips, Hides, Pelts and Skins.

#### 35 Water St., Norwich, Conn.

Western Department, 33 North Canal Street, Chicago, Ill.

# The Richmond Stove Company,

### MANUFACTURERS OF THE CELEBRATED

## Richmond Ranges,

## Richmond Stoves,

## Richmond Furnaces,

## Richmond Victor Steam Heaters.

### OFFICE AND FOUNDRY,

## Nos. 120 to 170 Thames Street,

### NORWICH, CONN.

# PRESTON BROS.,

### WHOLESALE AND RETAIL DEALERS IN

# HARDWARE,

### AND

# House-Furnishing Goods,

33 and 37 Shetucket Street and 162 Water Street, Norwich, Conn.

-:-  Oldest Hardware House in New London County.  -:-

# A. W. PRENTICE & CO.,

### JOBBERS AND RETAILERS OF

# Hardware, Cordage, Cutlery,

## Mill Supplies, Machinists' Tools, Carpenters'.

### Carriage Makers' and Blacksmiths' Materials,

## ELECTRIC BELLS, GAS LIGHTERS AND SUPPLIES,

### Fire Arms, Ammunition, Fishing Tackle, &c.

Agents for Howe's Scales, Hoyt's Belting, Dupont's Celebrated Gunpowder, and Miner's Friend Dynamite.

## 3, 5 and 7 Commerce Street. Norwich, Conn.

AMOS W. PRENTICE. LUTHER S. EATON.

# JOHN P. BARSTOW & CO.,

### DEALERS IN

# Stoves, Furnaces, Ranges,

## Seeds, Farm Implements, and Fertilizers,

### No. 15 Water Street, Norwich, Conn.

John P. Barstow. Frank H. Smith. George S. Byles.

ESTABLISHED 1843.

# L. W. CARROLL & SON,

## Commission Merchants,

AND DEALERS IN

# WOOL, COTTON,

## Manufacturers' Supplies, Dye Stuffs, Acids,

### BURLAPS, TWINES, STARCH,

## Paints, Oils, Glass, &c.

Nos. 17, 19 and 21 Water St., Norwich, Ct.

---

# CHARLES OSGOOD & CO.,

# WHOLESALE DRUGGISTS

AND DEALERS IN

## Patent Medicines,
### Masury's Railroad Colors,
## White Lead,
### Painter's Supplies,

### KEROSENE OIL, CHIMNEYS AND BURNERS.

PROPRIETORS OF

## OSGOOD'S STEAMBOAT OIL--Water White--150° Test.

### 45 and 47 Commerce St., Norwich, Ct.

# LEE & OSGOOD,

## WHOLESALE AND RETAIL

# DRUGGISTS,

129, 131 and 133 Main Street, and 150 and
152 Water Street, Norwich, Conn.,

## DEALERS IN

# Kerosene Oil,
# Chemicals,
# Acids,
# Paints,
# Oils,
# Varnishes,
# Window Glass,
# Brushes,
# Popular Patent Medicines

## AND

# MINERAL SPRING WATERS.

Established 1869.

# Duggan's Pharmacy,

### 50 Main Street, Norwich, Conn.

We offer to Physicians and the Public the services of careful and competent Apothecaries.

---

# JOHN M. BREWER,

### FRANKLIN SQUARE.

## Dealer in Drugs, Medicines, Chemicals,

### Fine Toilet Soaps, Brushes, Combs, Perfumery,

### AND FANCY TOILET ARTICLES IN GREAT VARIETY.

Physician's Prescriptions accurately compounded.

---

# BURRILL A. HERRICK,

# Wauregan House Pharmacy,

### Corner Broadway and Main St., Norwich, Conn.

## PURE DRUGS.        LOW PRICES.

---

## N. DOUGLAS SEVIN,

# Druggist, Dispensing Chemist.

*Wholesale and Retail Dealer in Chemicals, Patent Medicines, Perfumery, Fine Wines and Liquors,*

Brushes, Combs, Soaps, Chamois Skins, Sponges, Trusses, Mineral Waters, Champagne, London Porter, Scotch Ale.

**Special attention given to the proper application of Trusses, Supporters, Elastic Hose, &c.**

**118 Main Street, Norwich, Conn.**

# B. P. LEARNED,

# INSURANCE in all branches

**BONDS OF INDEMNITY** for Employers, Executors, Agents, Trustees, &c.
**FOREIGN DRAFTS** and **LETTERS OF CREDIT.**
**VALUABLE PACKAGES** by Registered Post or Express, Insured
at Low Rates of Premium.

Office, 20 Shetucket Street, over Thames National Bank.

---

# JOHN F. PARKER,

## FIRE AND MARINE

# INSURANCE AGENCY

Room No. 3 Chelsea Savings Bank Building,
SHETUCKET ST., NORWICH, CT.

Telephone Connection.

---

# J. F. WILLIAMS & SON,

# Fire and Marine Insurance,

## 91 MAIN STREET, NORWICH, CONN.

REPRESENTING THE OLDEST AND MOST RELIABLE STOCK AND MUTUAL
COMPANIES, INCLUDING THE

———SUN FIRE OFFICE, OF LONDON.———

THE OLDEST FIRE INSURANCE COMPANY IN THE WORLD.

J. F. WILLIAMS.                    J. H. WILLIAMS.

---

# A. IRVING ROYCE,

# -:- FIRE INSURANCE -:-

Office, over Thames National Bank, Shetucket Street, Norwich, Conn.

COMPANIES REPRESENTED: Phœnix, Hartford; Meriden, Meriden; People's, Middletown; Security, New Haven; German American, N. Y.; Niagara, N. Y.;
Continental, N. Y.; Commercial Union, London; London Assurance, London; Liverpool and London and Globe.

ESTABLISHED 1840.

# EDWARD CHAPPELL & CO.,

# LUMBER AND COAL,

## WHOLESALE AND RETAIL.

*Telephone Connection.*     46 to 76 W. Main St., Central Wharf, Norwich, Ct.

---

# JEWETT BROTHERS,

## LACKAWANNA COAL LEHIGH

Yard, 58 Thames St.     Branch Office, 154 Main St.

---

# E. D. HARRIS,

### DEALER IN

## Anthracite and Bituminous Coal.

Offices, 28 Broadway and 449 N. Main St., Norwich, Ct.

Telephone Connections.

---

# SETH L. PECK,

# MASON'S BUILDING MATERIALS.

## BRICK, CEMENT AND STONE.

### LIME FOR BUILDING, BLEACHING AND PAPER MAKING PURPOSES.

Sewer Pipe--Akron and Cement. Sheathing Paper, &c.

Central Wharf,    -    Norwich, Conn.

# N. S. GILBERT & SONS,

### WHOLESALE AND RETAIL DEALERS IN

# Furniture, Carpets, Wall Papers,

137 & 141 Main St., Norwich, Ct.

---

# DOYLE & MURPHY,

### WHOLESALE AND RETAIL DEALERS IN

# FURNITURE, OIL CLOTHS and CARPETS.

## Also, Furnishing Undertakers.

Furniture and Mattresses Re-upholstered and Made to Order.

*Nos. 37 and 41 Main St., Doyle's Block, Norwich.*

---

# A. W. DICKEY,

### DEALER IN

# FURNITURE,

## FEATHERS, MATTRESSES, MIRRORS, &c.,

26 and 28 Broadway.   -   Norwich, Conn.

---

# E. W. YERRINGTON,

### SOLE AGENT FOR

## Chickering & Sons' Pianos, and Loring & Blake's Organs.

Also, Pianos of several other reliable makers constantly in stock, and sold for
cash or installments, or rented on favorable terms.  Also,

## Carpets, Oil Cloths, Rugs, Mats, Mattings, Paper Hangings, Curtains, Borders

### At the Lowest Cash Prices.

E. W. YERRINGTON, 130 Main St.

7

# ROBERT BROWN,

## Steam and Gas Fitter and Plumber.

### AGENT FOR GORTON STEAM HEATERS.

### BRASS CASTINGS.

Pequot Building, Central Wharf, Norwich, Conn.

---

## GEORGE F. BARD,

## STEAM, GAS FITTER AND PLUMBER,

### BRASS FOUNDER AND COPPERSMITH.

Dealer in Wrought Iron Pipe, Fittings,
Valves, Engineers' Supplies, &c.,

24 Ferry Street,        -        Norwich, Conn.

---

## LANE BROS.,

# Manufacturers of Harness,

# Collars, Halters, &c.

### WHOLESALE AND RETAIL.

Junction Water and Commerce Sts., Norwich, Conn.

---

ESTABLISHED 1841.

# JOHN B. SHAW,

MANUFACTURER OF

# FINE HARNESS

AND DEALER IN

Trunks, Traveling Bags, Valises, Blankets, Whips, Saddles,

CARRIAGE ROBES, &c.,

213 Main Street, Franklin Square, Norwich, Ct.

# NOYES & DAVIS,

### WHOLESALE AND RETAIL DEALERS IN

# BOOKS, STATIONERY,

## Artists' Materials and Photographic Supplies,

152 and 154 Main Street, - Norwich, Conn.

---

# H. S. BATTIN,

## Books, Stationery, Artists' Materials,

## WINDOW SHADES AND PAPER HANGINGS,

### Wholesale and Retail.

## Next Door to Post Office. - Norwich, Conn.

---

Established in 1840.

F. T. CRANSTON. W. F. L. CRANSTON. L. H. CRANSTON.

# CRANSTON & CO.,

### (Formerly M. Safford & Co.) Jobbers and Retailers.

# Booksellers, Stationers and News Dealers,

## Artists' Materials and Photographic Outfits and Supplies.

*Telephone Connection.* *158 Main Street, Norwich, Conn.*

---

# CHAS. E. CHANDLER,

# CIVIL ENGINEER AND SURVEYOR,

161 Main St. Stafford N C

House Dr

BUY YOUR

# Clothing, Hats, Caps,

## AND FURNISHING GOODS

Of the reliable Combination Clothiers,

# F. A. WELLS & CO.,

84 Main Street, Norwich, Ct.

27 STORES.                27 STORES.

---

# Boston & Norwich Clothing Co.,

### 49 Main Street, Norwich, Conn.,

**DEALERS IN**

## FINE AND MEDIUM GRADE CLOTHING.

---

# HISLOP, PORTEOUS & MITCHELL,

**WHOLESALE AND RETAIL DEALERS IN**

# Dry and Fancy Goods,

## 93 and 95 Main Street,

Wholesale Entrances, 100 to 110 Water St.,

## NORWICH, CONN.

BRANCH HOUSES--New London, Conn.; Syracuse, N. Y.; Auburn, N. Y.;
Grand Rapids, Mich.

# THE BOSTON STORE, Reid & Hughes,

# DRY AND FANCY GOODS,

## Wholesale and Retail,

### 193 to 201 Main Street, Norwich, Ct.

---

# F. E. DOWE,

### DEALER IN

## Ladies' Dress and Wrap Trimmings, Hosiery, Kid Gloves,

### ARTISTIC EMBROIDERIES AND EMBROIDERY MATERIALS,

### 157 Main and 19 Shetucket Streets, Norwich, Conn.

### Summer Branch, "The Bazaar," at Watch Hill, R. I.

---

# C. C. BLISS,

# Watches, Clocks, Jewelry, Silver Ware,

## 126 Main St., Norwich, Ct.

---

# A. B. KINGSBURY,

# JEWELER.

## WATCHES, DIAMONDS, JEWELRY, PLATED WARE,

## Spectacles and Eye Glasses.

*I sell all makes of American Watches, and am Special Agent
for The F. A. Rogers Silver Co.*

### Cor. Broadway and Main St., Norwich.

# Franklin Steam Mills,

ESTABLISHED 1846.

## GEO. S. SMITH, Proprietor,

AND DEALER IN

Green and Roasted Coffees, Spices, Mustard, Cream Tartar
and Extracts. A FULL LINE OF FINE TEAS.

Sole Manufacturer of Palmer's Celebrated Dandelion Coffee.

*11—13 Commerce Street, Norwich, Conn.*

---

# STANTON & TYLER,

Wholesale and Retail Dealers in

# Teas, Coffees, Spices

## Mfrs. of Coffee Preparations from Cereals.

### 58 Main Street, Norwich, Conn.

---

# E. B. WORTHINGTON,

JOBBER IN

# TEAS, COFFEES, SPICES

## MUSTARD, CREAM TARTAR, &c.

### A FULL LINE OF TOBACCO AND CIGARS.

### 81 Water Street, Norwich, Conn.

---

## Estate of WILLIAM SPRAGUE,

WHOLESALE AND RETAIL DEALER IN

# Crockery, China, Glass

Silver Plated and Britannia Ware and House Furnishing Goods,

145 Main Street, Norwich, Conn.

A. D. SMITH.                    JOS. W. GILBERT.

# SMITH & GILBERT,

# Merchant Tailors

AND

## MEN'S FINE FURNISHINGS.

140 Main Street,   -   Norwich, Conn.

---

R. H. Jones & Son,

Merchant Tailors,

Chambers, 128 Main St., Norwich, Ct.

---

# CURRIER BROTHERS,

# -:Merchant Tailors,:-

### DEALERS IN

# Men's and Boys' Clothing,

No. 207 Main Street, Norwich, Conn.

---

# E. A. PRENTICE,

# HATTER, FURRIER & MEN'S FURNISHER

Has on hand a complete line of the above goods, at reasonable prices. Fur repairing and storing a specialty.

## None but First-Class Goods sold.

### A PLEASURE TO SHOW GOODS.

13 Broadway, Norwich, Conn.

# GEO. W. KIES & CO.,

### Wholesale and Retail Dealers in

# Boots, Shoes and Rubbers,

### 80 Main Street, Norwich, Conn., directly opposite Post Office.

GEO. W. KIES.                                           JAMES J. COTTLE.

---

### ESTABLISHED 1847.

# J. H. KELLEY,

### Dealer in Ladies', Misses' and Children's Shoes, and Men's and Boys'

## BOOTS AND SHOES of all grades,

### E. C. BURT & CO'S GOODS FOR LADIES,
### HATHAWAY, SOULE & HARRINGTON'S GOODS FOR MEN AND BOYS.

### Also, LEATHER AND SHOE FINDINGS, AND HARNESS LEATHER.

### No. 18 Franklin Square, Norwich, Conn.

---

# G. W. HAMILTON,

# Boots, Shoes and Rubbers.

*Our goods are bargains in quality and price. We warrant every pair of shoes we sell. Gents., ask for*

# HAMILTON'S $3.00 SHOE.

*Every pair cut from extra fine tannery calf Skins.*

### No. 134 Main Street,    -    -    Norwich, Conn.

---

# BOOTS AND SHOES.

## Fine Goods a Specialty.

*We keep in stock everything that can be found in a First-Class Boot and Shoe Store.*

OUR MOTTO--Best Value given every time for the Money.

## JAS. F. COSGROVE & CO., 206 Main St., Norwich, Conn.

# J. C. PERKINS,

## Confectionery Manufacturer,

*The Largest Confectionery Establishment in the state.*

Assortment embracing every variety of Candies known to the trade

### Wholesale and Retail.

**Perkins Block, Main Street,   -   Norwich, Conn.**

---

## CONNECTICUT POP CORN CO.,

*Manufacturers of Pop Corn and Corn Cakes in all the popular forms and flavors; also, of*

# CHOICE CONFECTIONERY,

*in every desirable flavor and shape, and nut and fruit combinations to meet the public demand,*
### WHOLESALE AND RETAIL.

Our prices are always the lowest market prices for the grade of goods offered. Orders by telegraph, mail or telephone promptly filled.

**C. H. NOYES, Agent.   Office, 58 Broadway, Norwich, Conn.**

---

# Real Estate Office.

Experience, Natural Tact, Honor and Enterprise

has won the Banner for this Agency.

## H. F. PALMER, 45 Main St., Norwich, Ct.

---

# N. TARRANT,

# REAL ESTATE AGENT

#### ESTABLISHED 1870.

### 45 Main Street,  -  Norwich, Conn.

# Woodworth & Small,
# DRUGS, CHEMICALS
## PAINTS, OILS, WINDOW GLASS.
Agents for H. W. John's Liquid Paint.
## NORWICH, CONN.

---

# THE S. F. BEER CO.,
### C. B. HARRINGTON, Proprietor,
## Manufacturers of GROCERS' SUPPLIES,
### AND WHOLESALE DEALERS IN VINEGAR,
17 Commerce Street, - Norwich, Conn.

---

# J. B. MERSHON,
#### Manufacturer and Wholesale and Retail Dealer in
## Imported Havana and Domestic Cigars,
### Tobacco, Pipes, Snuff and Smokers' Articles generally.
110 Main Street, Norwich, Conn.

---

# J. M. HUNTINGTON & CO.,

# IMPORTERS OF MOLASSES,
### AND
General Shipping and Commission Merchants.

# ARMOUR & CO.,

### DEALERS IN

## Chicago Dressed Beef, Mutton, Hogs, &c.

### Foot of Ferry St., Norwich, Conn.

---

# WINTERS, SWIFT & CO.,

### WHOLESALE DEALERS IN

## SWIFT'S CHICAGO DRESSED BEEF

### LAMB, MUTTON, PORK, TONGUES AND TRIPE,

*Sales Room and Office, opposite N. L. N. R. R. Depot, Norwich, Conn.*

---

# CASE & FULLER,

### WHOLESALE DEALERS IN

## Flour, Groceries, Butter, Cheese

### Foreign and Domestic Fruits,

*Nos. 45 to 51 Water Street,    -    -    Norwich, Conn.*

---

# L. A. GALLUP,

## Wholesale Dealer in Groceries and Fruits,

### AND COMMISSION MERCHANT.

### FINEST GRADES BUTTER AND CHEESE.

Burlaps, Starch, Bale Rope, and Mill Supplies to order a specialty

No. 31 Water Street,    -    Norwich, Conn.

Telephone Connection.

# R, S. BARTLETT,

### DEALER IN

## CHOICE FAMILY GROCERIES,

Always on hand, a full line of Choice Creamery Butter.

Sole Agent in Norwich for the "VIENNA HAXALL," Choice Red River Flour.

4 Main Street, (Breed Hall) Norwich, Conn.

---

# JOHN D. BREWSTER,

## DEALER IN FINE GROCERIES, FLOUR OF ALL GRADES,

### Selected Teas, Pure Coffees and Spices.

Butter and Cheese, from best Vermont and New York Dairies.

*Choice Syrup and Molasses, Foreign and Domestic Fruits. Canned Fruits in variety.*

Also, a complete assortment of Goods usually kept in a First-Class Store.

*Goods delivered promptly, free of expense.*

---

# W. H. CARDWELL,

## Wholesale and Retail Dealer in Groceries, Provisions, Flour,

### CANNED GOODS, &c.,

*Nos. 3 to 9 MARKET STREET, NORWICH, CONN.*

Highly important it is that new-comers to our city should know that W. H. CARDWELL, Nos. 3 to 9 Market Street, is one of its live grocers. This means business, and that is its length, breadth and thickness.

---

# F. L. GARDNER,

### DEALER IN

## FINE ✛ GROCERIES ✛ AND ✛ TEAS,

### Provisions, Flour, Grain, Fruit, Wooden Ware, &c.,

Corner Market and Water Streets,    -    Norwich, Conn.

# A. T. OTIS,

## Dealer in Groceries, Flour, Fruit,

AND AN ASSORTMENT OF

# CANNED GOODS,

261 Main Street, - - Norwich, Conn.

---

# H. D. RALLION,

# GROCER,

## No. 10 Broadway, Norwich, Conn.

## Fine Goods a Specialty.

---

ESTABLISHED IN 1868.

# JOHN F. SEVIN,

DEALER IN

# Groceries, Provisions and Yankee Notions

190 and 192 East Broad Street, Norwich, Conn.

---

# O. H. REYNOLDS,

## -:- Hack, Livery and Boarding Stable, -:-

Nos. 55, 57 and 59 Shetucket St., Norwich, Ct.

Carriages furnished for Funerals, Parties and Weddings.

*Orders by Telegraph, Telephone or Mail, promptly attended to.*

# PAGE STEAM HEATING CO.,

## MANUFACTURERS OF THE

# Page Low Pressure

# Steam Boiler.

### ALSO,

## Standard Hot Water Heater,

Correspondence Solicited.

Address W. C. MOWRY, Treas., Lock Box 1163, Norwich, Conn.

---

# THE NORWICH MALT CO.,

## 10 to 20 WEST MAIN STREET.

### INCORPORATED 1886.

ANDREW WIGGIN, President and General Manager.
JOHN W. FREE, Vice President.
J. B. COMSTOCK, Secretary and Treasurer.

The only place in the United States where **MALT** is now made by
continuous malting, by

## Machinery under Patents owned by JOHN W. FREE.

Brewers, Maltsters, and others interested in improvements
are invited to call and examine the process of manufacturing. Samples sent to any part of the
country on application.

# J. P. COLLINS & CO.,

BUILDERS OF

# Turbine Water Wheels,

**Both Horizontal and Vertical, together with Heavy Connecting Machinery.**

# The "CRANSTON"
# PRINTING PRESSES.

Printers, Publishers and Stationers contemplating purchase of a Cylinder Printing Press are invited to investigate the merits of the "Cranston."

IT IS IN EVERY RESPECT A SUPERIOR PRESS. ·—·

—·· EVERY REASONABLE GUARANTEE GIVEN WITH IT.

Catalogue, Price List and full information furnished promptly upon application to the manufacturer.

## J. H. CRANSTON,  -  Norwich, Conn.

Any further information that may be had
ing the Facilities to be obtained at the
Mechanical or Transportation P
fully furnished by addressing  C
of the Norwich B
H H CA

www.ingramcontent.com/pod-product-compliance
Lightning Source LLC
Chambersburg PA
CBHW030847270326
41928CB00007B/1251

* 9 7 8 3 3 3 7 4 3 0 3 6 8 *